FINDING DAVEY

A Father's Search for His Son in the Afterlife

David R. Alison III

Foreword by Suzanne Giesemann

Dedication

This is for you, Davey

Finding Davey
By David R. Alison III

www.findingdavey.com

International Standard Book Number: 978-1-7326670-0-6

Contents

Foreword 7

Introduction 11

I Can't Imagine 13

Meeting Davey 16

Gathering the Family 19

Surviving the Quake 22

Synchronicity 26

The Five of Us..28

I'm So Sorry 30

Achieving Goals 33

Riding the Waves 35

The Family Business 37

Changing Course 40

Awakening 48

Fleeting Joy 51

Talking to Davey 54

Connections...60

Davey's Gift 64

Family...66

Reintegrating 70

Friends..74

Digital Landmines...79

Signs 83

Finding Mediums..90

Beginning Meditation..93

250 Days 97

Reflections on My Father 101

An Engineer's Dilemma 105

Seeing Davey Again 110

Growing Together 115

Helping Parents Heal 120

Allison's Reading 122

Continuing Messages 127

Transformations 132
    Spirituality 133
    Mindfulness 134
    Judgment 135
    Death and Dying 137
    Getting Through Each Day 139

Epilogue 142

Foreword

If one were to stereotype an engineer, certain characteristics come to mind: analytical, logical, methodical, science-based, and no-nonsense. The author of this book, David Alison, typifies all of those terms. But David Alison is also a loving husband and father, and it is this identity that led him to write this moving book. As the result of the death of his son, Davey, David had the impetus and the courage to go where many men and most engineers dare not venture: into the world of the unseen and the unproven.

I had the honor and pleasure of meeting Davey before I met his father. I got to know Davey during a one-hour session conducted with David's wife, Allison. I am an evidential medium, and Allison contacted me in hopes of connecting with Davey across the veil. As you will read later in this book, we did exactly that. Davey is an outstanding communicator with a vibrant spirit, who made the session with him easier than most.

With my background as a Navy commander and commanding officer, I can identify with David's left-brain mentality. Having endured the sudden death of my stepdaughter Susan, I can also identify with what a family goes through when a child crosses the veil—Susan's passing caused me to embark on a journey quite similar to David's. I can promise you, David's grief did not make him lose his grip on reality. Quite the opposite. Because of Davey's passing, David has discovered a greater reality.

This book serves as a primer for parents with a child who has transitioned. It is especially important and valuable for men, particularly fathers, who are grieving. Parts of the Alison family's story are difficult to read. Please do not put the book down or skip the painful parts that describe the events surrounding Davey's passing. They are integral to David's motivation in writing this book. At the risk of stereotyping again, I will say that for a man, David has done an excellent job of describing the emotional trauma he and his family suffered. Since he has shared his feelings and experiences so openly, readers in a similar situation will know that they are not the only ones going through such trauma. All will understand why David stretched himself beyond his comfort zone and traditional worldview to do as the title suggests and *find Davey*.

It has been proven that by reading stories of others' experiences, we are more likely to have such experiences of our own. David Alison shares here a multitude of signs and encounters he has enjoyed with Davey since his son's transition. In my classes and workshops, I teach methods to increase the likelihood of such experiences, and I can assure you that the events you will read about can be believed and trusted.

I have sat with thousands of people in grief. Most want desperately to have the kind of experiences David describes in this book, but few achieve this level and quantity of interaction. This is a testament to David's discipline and dedication and to Davey's powerful soul.

David and Allison are outstanding examples of Shining Light Parents. This is a new term that we hope you will share with others after reading *Finding Davey*. A Shining Light Parent is one whose child has left the physical body, but whose light continues to shine as an ongoing presence in the family's heart and home.

The term is a positive replacement for the term "bereaved parent," reflecting an awareness that the light of the soul cannot be extinguished on *either* side of the veil. "Shining Light Parent" carries different meanings depending on where one is in the healing process:

- As one begins the healing journey after a passing, it is the child in spirit—like Davey—who is the Shining Light. It is their light that keeps us going.
- Moment by moment, thanks to unmistakable signs from those across the veil, undeniable synchronicities, and support from others, those still in physical form begin to feel the light within themselves once again.
- With the help of the Shining Lights across the veil, those here who are doing the challenging work of healing after a passing begin to serve as shining examples for those new to the journey. The child who has passed rejoices in this healing. It no longer feels right to call such people "bereaved parents." Like David and Allison, they have graduated to full status as "Shining Light Parents."

If you are a bereaved parent and look forward to being able to call yourself a Shining Light Parent, by all means follow David's examples: Read books on the afterlife. Go to conferences about the afterlife. Attend workshops or classes with those who legitimately and regularly connect across the veil. Meditate or practice presence regularly. Seek guidance from and ask questions of Higher Consciousness. Constantly check your belief system: is it helping or hindering you? Be open to the signs your loved ones are sending you. When you receive an undeniable sign or a visit from your loved one, honor that! Talk to your Shining Lights often and know that they hear you. Most of all, as David Alison so courageously demonstrates, don't worry what others think or say. It's not their journey. It's yours.

Finding Davey shows that it is possible to heal from the death of a child. The light of the soul may grow dim temporarily as we face life's inevitable challenges, but that spark never goes out. May we celebrate the eternal life of Davey and all of those who have passed by making every effort to turn up our lights in their honor.

Suzanne Giesemann
Author and Evidential Medium

Introduction

I am writing this book because I've been given a tremendous gift. This may sound odd coming from a father who lost his 24 year old son in an automobile accident. After my son passed I found myself desperately searching for him, asking myself: He couldn't really be gone, could he? Was that it?

My goal with this work is simple: to help parents who have lost a child to heal and to help their friends and family members gain a new perspective, to better help their loved ones. Feeling that I wasn't alone while mired in the deepest tragedy I ever faced was critical to my healing.

If you have recently lost someone you care about and are in the throes of grief, it is my desire that this book will help you know that it's going to be okay. The grief of losing a child is devastating and while all may seem hopeless in the early stages, it is possible to recover from this if you open your mind and give yourself time. In these pages I share the lessons I've learned and the tools I've found that helped me to not only learn to live with the loss of my son but to actually find a ray of hope, to laugh again, and to see my world in a completely new and beautiful way.

You will walk directly in my footsteps. I will share with you the depth of my sorrow and the pinnacle of my joy. You will know my mind-set and perspective and to a large degree see how I have processed what's happened. My hope is that some of this will resonate directly with you and that you too will gain a new perspective on life and see how amazing everything can be again once you embrace the change that is needed.

This is, after all a love story and with that you now have mine.

I Can't Imagine

July 20, 2016

I knew something was very, very wrong. It was one of those deep in the gut feelings—a premonition. My son, Davey, had said he was going to drive to River Bend Park for a trail run but that was five hours ago. I texted him a few times asking him to text or call to let me know he was okay, but there had been no response.

Our entire family has iPhones, so when you send a message you can get a little "Delivered" confirmation—an indication that at least the person I was sending it to had their phone on and were receiving messages. When I sent the messages to Davey's phone that day, they came back as "Sent as SMS"—I knew that meant that his phone was not receiving the messages or he was completely out of range.

My wife, Allison, arrived home just a couple hours after Davey left. On her way home the traffic was completely backed up, so she took a shortcut—the same road that led to River Bend Park. Just a couple miles down that road she found that the passage had been blocked; there was an unoccupied police car and a wooden barrier forcing cars to turn around. It appeared there was an accident on the road ahead: around a curve but out of her sight.

Allison would later tell me that she felt tremendous anxiety as she sat in her car wondering about the cause of the road block. She considered getting out and walking down the road to see what had happened but a voice told her to turn around and get home quickly. Her phone was broken and she couldn't call me so she decided to turn around and drive home using another road.

13

Panic gripped her and when she arrived home to find that Davey had left a couple hours earlier she insisted I call the police to see if they had any details about that accident.

I called the police and they would only tell me that the accident Allison had come upon earlier involved a solo car and they didn't have any other details. I gave them my contact information as well as a description of Davey's car and the license plate number; they said they would notify the local patrol officers to look for him.

It was now early evening and still Davey had not returned. As the sun slowly went down on that summer day I sat in the front of our house, moving a chair so that I had an unobstructed view of the long strip of driveway that led up to our front door. Allison and our oldest daughter, Jocelyn, were in the backyard, pacing around, also worried about Davey.

Suddenly I saw a vehicle pull up to our house. It wasn't Davey's older Volvo sedan; it was a large, dark SUV. It pulled in and another SUV, a twin to the first, pulled in behind it.

I ran outside, yelling to the girls that someone was here. We converged on the SUVs just as two men got out of the vehicles. The younger of the two men, wearing a Fairfax County, Virginia, police uniform, asked me if I owned a 2001 Volvo sedan. As I tried to stumble out a response Allison started to frantically yell "Just tell me if he's OKAY!!! Is he OKAY???" The older of the two police officers then offered that the car had been in a solo vehicle accident and had hit a tree.

Everything went into slow motion. I told them my son had been driving the car and the older officer slowly said "I'm sorry, but the driver did not make it."

At this point my world went numb. Allison cried out a loud "No!" and the light she normally had in her eyes seemed to just go out. My daughter started to cry uncontrollably. I had difficulty standing and lowered myself to the driveway. It had to be a mistake. Davey would pull up any moment and clear up the confusion.

My only thought at this point was that this couldn't be happening. It wasn't real. That thought just kept going through my mind. I didn't cry at first. All I wanted to do was scream "NO!"

I regained a little of my composure and switched into a numb autopilot mode. Nothing seemed real anymore and I had this deep pain inside my body. It was like a blackness that was slowly expanding and consuming me. All the thoughts I normally had going on in my head—tasks I needed to do, planning for the future, business issues…everything just stopped and exited my head. All I could think about was one name:

Davey.
Davey.
Davey.

I mentally repeated his name over and over again in my mind. I was engulfed in this inky blackness and my son's name was the only thing I could think of.

One of the police officers asked me if I had a photo of my son. I grabbed my iPhone and pulled up a still frame from a video I had taken just a few days earlier, hoping that he would tell me it wasn't him. He looked at the face on the screen and then carefully handed back my phone.

"Yes. That's him."

Meeting Davey

October 23, 1991

In late October of 1991, I got to see the first image of the child Allison was pregnant with. We had gone to get an ultrasound at the four-month mark to check on the progress of our baby.

As the doctor ran the ultrasound scanner over Allison's belly she saw something. She asked if we wanted to know the gender of our baby and we quickly said yes! She pointed to something on the screen and said "Right there—see? You are going to have a boy."

I looked up at Allison and said "I'm going to have a son?!?"

The look in Allison's eyes brought a tear to mine. I was beside myself with joy and stared at the image of my son that was printed out from the ultrasound machine, tracing over the outline and trying to figure out what he would look like.

Our life up to this point had been like a fairy tale. Our daughter, Jocelyn, was two and a half years old and was a complete blessing.

I had grown up with a single brother and all male cousins and so had spent the past couple years learning how to handle little girl issues. Jocelyn was the first girl in our extended family and she had been showered with special attention. From frilly dresses to Barbie dolls and Puffalumps, I was in new territory.

Now it would be different—I was going to have a son! I would know exactly what to do in every situation (or so I naively thought). There was no question what his name would be: David Reese Alison IV. The only challenge was what to call him. My grandfather went by David but he was estranged from our family and I never had contact with him. My dad went by Dave and I occasionally did too, but Allison insisted on calling me David to differentiate me from my dad. Calling a little guy Dave seemed odd so we decided on Davey.

The name would end up fitting him perfectly.

Davey was born on March 20, 1992, and his entry into our lives was not without challenges. Jocelyn had been born complication-free and we expected the same with our son's birth. Allison had an epidural to help with pain management and about six hours into labor she suddenly developed a rather large uterine band, a constriction in her uterus that was effectively squeezing Davey before he could be delivered.

Alarms began to sound as the probe the nurse had attached to Davey indicated he was going into fetal distress. The doctor came in and quickly recommended that an emergency C-section be performed to deliver our son.

Allison was quickly wheeled into an operating room and prepped for surgery. Within five minutes an incision had been made and Davey's head was popping out of the lower part of Allison's abdomen. A nurse quickly cleared Davey's mouth and nose and he immediately started to cry, while only partially out of Allison's belly.

The moment was surreal because, while this was happening, Allison started to have difficulty breathing. Apparently the epidural they had administered was affecting her lungs and she was struggling to breathe. She alternated between crying out "How's the baby?" and "I can't breathe!" I was in full panic mode, worried about losing both my new son and my wife within just a few minutes.

It took a while for Allison's breathing to return to normal, but Davey stabilized very quickly and appeared perfectly healthy. Allison's recovery was significantly longer than it had been after Jocelyn was born, but within a few days I was able to bring both of them home.

Davey put on weight quickly and was a chunky little dude with the cutest smile ever. I still vividly remember taking my four-month-old son downstairs early in the morning so that Allison could sleep. I'd lay out a little blanket on the floor and place him there on his back and he would just look at me and make little baby noises as the sun rose outside. I was completely fascinated with him.

I had grown up in Southern California and still lived there, and my mom, dad, and brother all lived there as well. Allison's family had moved to California from Virginia about a decade earlier and her three siblings also lived nearby. Our extended family was becoming rather large and we all got together nearly every weekend.

By late 1993 our two children had five cousins that were within a few years of each other, and they were all very close. From visits to Disneyland to just hanging out at different parks or houses, we traveled as a large pack. There was always something to do, somewhere to go, and a dozen of us together.

Gathering the Family

July 20, 2016

My world had collapsed. The police officers had left and Allison, Jocelyn, and I went to our backyard. Jocelyn's dog Holtby — a young Golden Retriever — was there. Each of us cried and held one another as Holtby kept nuzzling against our bodies, trying to comfort us. Normally he would just be running around in the backyard but he clearly sensed our distress and was trying desperately to provide us comfort.

I was amazed how tender he was to each of us. It was as though he truly understood what was happening and was giving us loving support.

It fell on me to start notifying our extended family about what had happened. I got in touch with my sister-in-law Jeanne first. I could barely get the words out of my mouth: "Davey died in a car accident..." Jeanne completely lost it, immediately crying and yelling out "NO!"

I kept the call brief because as it created an even more unbearable pain than that I was already in. Next I called my mother-in-law, Joyce. She had been at our house a few days earlier and had just flown back to California. Davey had driven her to the airport when she left. I asked her to notify the rest of the family for me so that I wouldn't have to keep reliving this and fortunately for me she took on that responsibility.

There was one person I did need to talk to desperately — my younger brother, Daryl. Though he lived in California and I in Virginia, we are very close and speak on the phone nearly every day. I broke the news to him and he managed to keep his composure while trying his best to comfort me. I didn't realize at that moment that Daryl would become the rock I would lean on heavily over the course of the days and weeks ahead.

Within hours of the news going out, dozens of family members and friends were on flights from all over the country, trying to get to us as quickly as possible. Allison's brother, Tom was able to get a flight but his wife and four kids could not, so the five of them jumped into their SUV and started driving from Houston, Texas, to our house to be with us.

Our youngest daughter, Julia, was in Bethany Beach, Delaware, for the summer working at Mango's, a restaurant on the boardwalk. It was difficult to reach her and I didn't want her to receive that call on her own, at work. Fortunately two of our dear friends, Barbara and Kathi, had been visiting Allison and staying at our beach house with her but had stayed in Bethany after Allison left, unaware of what was unfolding back at our home. I was able to reach them and asked them to tell Julia what had happened and bring her home. They went to Mango's and broke the news to our daughter, then drove her back to our home in Virginia.

Julia was just six days away from her twenty-first birthday. Davey had been planning to leave for the beach and spend all of the next week with her celebrating; the two of them had become very close over the last few years and Julia had been planning "Juliapalooza" for months.

The knowledge that so many of our friends and family were making their way to us was comforting but there was no escaping the pain of what we were experiencing; I continued to have a deep numb feeling clouding my mind, and my body felt wracked with a dull pain that I couldn't place—it was all over my body. I continued to repeat a single name over and over again:

Davey.

Surviving the Quake

January 17, 1994

Our young family would face a major challenge on January 17, 1994, at our home in Northridge, California. At 4:30 a.m. a 6.7-magnitude earthquake kicked off — its epicenter about eight blocks south of our home. Having grown up in Southern California, I had experienced my share of earthquakes, but being that close to the epicenter of such a strong quake was terrifying. The initial shock of the quake threw me and Allison completely out of bed.

Allison ran to Davey's room and pulled him from his crib and I ran into Jocelyn's room and picked her up. The house was shaking violently and I found Jocelyn curled in a ball in the middle of her bed — all of her furniture had fallen over. Her tall dresser had struck her bed and I couldn't believe it hadn't hit her.

We huddled in the doorways of our children's two rooms, waiting for it to stop. Though the initial quake technically only lasted about twenty seconds, our house continued to shake for at least ten minutes as minor aftershocks rolled in.

Once the quake finally came to an end, I ventured downstairs to assess the damage. Most of our windows had broken from the house twisting and buckling. The kitchen was a shambles, with every dish and glass out of the cabinets, most broken and on the floor. The refrigerator had tipped over, spilling the contents on the floor; a six pack of beer in it had hit the floor with enough force to pop open the cans and spray their contents everywhere. Outside, our brick chimney had toppled over and the cinderblock walls bordering our yard had collapsed.

As we made our way outside we could hear people yelling and screaming. The predawn sky contained half a dozen small sunrises—nearby homes that had caught fire immediately after the earthquake. We checked in on our neighbors and found that everyone on our street had escaped with just minor cuts and bruises.

I grabbed our big clunky VHS video camera and filmed the house once it became light, my voice cracking with emotion as I recounted how lucky we were that our house didn't completely collapse like some of the homes just a few blocks away. Many of the deaths in that earthquake occurred less than a mile from us. A large three-story apartment complex had been reduced to two stories in height; the bottom floor had collapsed and sixteen people had lost their lives.

While we were fine physically, the challenges of living in Northridge had just begun. Without phones, power, water, or gas, our house wasn't really habitable. We packed up our car with some clothes and slowly made our way to Allison's parent's house in Westlake Village, normally a forty-minute drive away—a much longer trip now, since the freeway overpasses had collapsed. We drove by the shopping center we frequented regularly; the entire parking structure had collapsed and the rest of the building showed signs of extensive damage.

The next five months were a blur. We were fortunate that we had earthquake insurance and were able to quickly get our house repaired. But while the damage to our home had been fixed, the earthquake had wreaked havoc with the value of our house. Though we had made a significant down payment when we bought the home and made many renovations and updates, the value was suddenly below what we still owed on the mortgage after five years in a growing real estate market.

The constant aftershocks made living in the house unbearable for us, so we moved in to Allison's parent's house after ours was repaired and rented ours out to another family while their house was being completely rebuilt.

Allison's formative years—middle school, high school, and college—had all been spent in Virginia. She moved to California after college to attend Pepperdine Law School but always spoke fondly of Virginia. With the earthquake suddenly uprooting our home, Allison wanted to move back to the Commonwealth. In May of 1994 Allison and I flew out to Northern Virginia to check it out. I fell in love with it immediately.

I am a native Angeleno, born and raised in Los Angeles County. While I had traveled a bit in the US, I had never been to Virginia and honestly didn't know what to expect. If you haven't seen Virginia in late spring, you are missing out on one of the most beautiful parts of the country.

Fortunately, as an experienced software engineer I could pretty much find a job anywhere I wanted to live—Northern Virginia in the mid-1990s was no problem. I sent out some résumés, got immediate responses, and flew out to Virginia for interviews. In a few days I had three job offers, each with full relocation packages and a salary that was comparable to what I was making in California, even though the cost of living was lower.

Moving away from our extended family was a very difficult decision. With both of our parents in easy driving range and all of the brothers, sisters, and cousins so close, we were about to move to the other side of the country with only some distant family members there to back us up.

Allison and I looked at it as a huge adventure. I was married to a woman I adored, had two beautiful kids and complete job security. If anyone could move to the other side of the country and start fresh, we could.

Synchronicity

July 21, 2016

The last thing on my mind was planning a memorial service for my son. Frankly I was still in disbelief that Davey had passed. With dozens of people already on flights or in the middle of long drives to get to our home, it became apparent we needed to put something together within a couple days. Though both Allison and I were raised Catholic and each of our children had been baptized, we had drifted away from the church over the years.

Some of our friends took charge and arranged for a venue: Crossroads Methodist Church opened their doors for us. We had been there several times for services over the years and the church housed the nursery school each of our children attended so it was very familiar to us.

We needed someone to run the service, and Allison immediately thought of Tom Rockwood. Tom had been Davey's Young Life leader during high school and was also his lacrosse coach. Over the years our families had become good friends, though Tom was closer to our kids' age than our own.

A few years earlier Tom had moved with his young family to Ohio and we hadn't spoken in a couple years—Instagram and Facebook had kept us connected, though. I was going to have to call Tom and break the news to him about Davey, and ask him if he would be able to drive out to Virginia on ridiculously short notice and honor Davey at his memorial service.

I called Tom and he answered immediately. I broke down as I told him that Davey had died the day before in an accident.

"That can't be! I'm meeting with him this afternoon!"

I was shocked to hear this. Tom explained: He'd had some text conversations with Davey just the day before, on the morning of the accident. It turned out Tom was already in Virginia, running a lacrosse camp just a few miles from our house, and he and Davey were planning on getting together the next day. We chatted for a bit and Tom quickly agreed that he would facilitate Davey's memorial service.

This was just the first of many little things that lined up in ways that we didn't expect over the next few weeks. I had the feeling these moments were far more than a series of random coincidences.

The Five of Us

July 26, 1995

After we had been in Virginia for nearly a year, our little Julia Rose was born. Julia came to us five weeks early and spent her first week in the NICU, which terrified us initially. Though she was a tiny little five-pound baby she was, and still is, a fighter. Once she came home she quickly put on weight and became a healthy, happy baby.

Watching our kids grow up, it became increasingly clear that Jocelyn and Julia were unique and outgoing girls that sometimes rubbed each other the wrong way, but Davey was in between them in age and could relate to both very easily. When you put the three of them together everything just worked. I liked to say that Jocelyn and Julia were complex math equations and Davey was the equal sign in the middle of them.

It was a crazy time, having three young children under one roof. Allison and I were stretched pretty thin but our little family was complete and I didn't think I could be any happier.

As the kids started to get older I loved to play games with them. Our favorite was "Gorilla"—I would turn on our stereo and play the Disney *Tarzan* soundtrack by Phil Collins. As the music built up to a crescendo I would pretend to turn into a gorilla and the kids would all scream and hide. Once the drums started I would chase each through the house, tickling any that came within my grasp.

I clearly remember coming home from work: the kids would run up to me, give me massive hugs, and then sit on my feet, wrapped around my legs, making me walk around with them.

We had dinner together nearly every night and I got to spend a lot of quality time with my family.

Though I had an extremely successful career as a software engineer, the role I most identified with was being a father. As a child my mom had been the active and loving parent in our home, and she was the model I used for my own kids. My dad was around and occasionally engaged with my brother and me, but his alcoholism kept him pretty detached. I was determined not to make that same mistake with my children and was thrilled to be an active part of their lives as they grew up.

Each of our kids played sports: soccer was the big one. All three children played, and I signed up to coach. I soon was spending all of my non-work hours coaching each of the teams our children played on and volunteering to help manage our local youth football league.

It was exhausting but worth it. Not only was I getting to spend quality time with my kids, I got to know hundreds of kids in our community. Between Allison being a teacher in our local high school and me coaching almost every sport the kids played, the two of us knew the majority of the families with children in town. I felt deeply linked to an ever-increasing number of people, and that sense of connection seemed to make everything a bit easier.

I'm So Sorry

July 22, 2016

As our friends and family began to show up at our house during the two days after Davey's accident we learned one of the most difficult parts about the early stages of a traumatic event like this: our closest friends and family were grieving too and nobody seemed to know how to deal with us.

Nearly every person that I embraced broke down and began to cry. "I'm so sorry" was a constant refrain I heard over and over again. Some of the most stoic men I know had a brave face on when approaching me but as soon as I embraced them their bodies began to wrack with sobs. Tough men—military veterans that had seen combat and suffered loss—would be overcome. They would quickly recover but by that point another friend or family member would be in front of me and the process would start again.

Another phrase I heard often was one that I had said myself when a friend lost his teenage son: "I can't imagine." Now they were likely doing the same thing I had done when my friend's son died: trying to imagine how they would deal with a loss so great.

In the past, when I'd heard of a young person's death, I would immediately think of my own children. How could I keep them safe? My mom was worried all the time when I was growing up and I inherited that trait; I worried for my children with the incorrect intent of helping to prevent the worst from happening to them. What I was really doing was projecting my fear onto my kids.

In those early days after Davey died, I quickly realized that I needed to repress my own grief and be strong for the friends and family that were there to support me. I put myself on autopilot again; the muscles on my face relaxed to the point where I had a detached look, my eyes staring off into the distance until someone approached me and I had to interact with them.

I was a complete mess. I hadn't eaten anything in the two days since the accident. I was drinking a lot of water though—the constant crying dehydrated me completely. On Friday morning I stepped on the scale in our bathroom and was shocked to see that I had lost eight pounds. Though Allison and I retreated to our bedroom to get some quiet when we could, sleep eluded me. When I closed my eyes all I could think of was a single name, repeated over and over again:

Davey.

I looked at my wife of thirty years and saw the immense pain in her face. My daughters alternated between looking like adults trying to help us in our grief and little girls that just needed their mom and dad. I felt like my family was in free fall and we were missing someone. Davey couldn't really be gone—he just couldn't be. This wasn't real.

I never felt like he was gone. It felt like he was still in the house. Was this just how grief manifested? Was I in denial? Why did I feel like he was still around us?

Though I spent the majority of my time in our bedroom, I had not slept at all in two full days. I was lying in bed very late at night on the day before Davey's memorial service, staring up at the ceiling. Suddenly I saw an incredibly bright white light—though it wasn't a light in the traditional sense. It didn't cast shadows and it didn't appear to have a single source. I had never seen anything like it.

I then heard a voice very clearly say:

"It's okay, you can sleep."

Suddenly I felt complete peace. The inky blackness that had consumed me was replaced by a feeling of comfort and security that I didn't think was even possible. For the next eight hours I dropped into a wonderfully peaceful and dreamless slumber that my body desperately needed.

Achieving Goals

June 1, 1998

As our family grew, so too did our good fortune. I always had an entrepreneurial side, and being a software engineer in the late '90s, when the Internet was just starting to take off, was the perfect time to branch out on my own. Allison had been working part time as a lawyer while spending most of her time raising the kids, though she decided she would like to switch careers and become a public high school teacher. With three young children at home and Allison going to school for her masters in education, I decided to take the leap into self-employment.

We didn't really have a financial safety net. I was able to land a decent software consulting contract that provided us with regular income, but what I really wanted to spend my time on was a new product I had developed. WebSurveyor was one of the early entries in online surveying, and in the months leading up to its release I had spent all my evenings and weekends in the basement working on it. I launched it in June of 1998, and with it some expenses that required me to rack up some significant credit card debt.

Over the late '90s and into the early 2000s, Tom Lueker and Bruce Mancinelli joined the WebSurveyor team, and we managed to get an angel round of funding to help fuel the growth of the business. Fortunately for me I chose some outstanding partners, and together we hired some amazing people that took the business forward. By 2004 we were hitting the Inc. 500 for the fastest-growing privately held companies—and by 2006 we had gotten offers to acquire the company.

Even though I didn't really want to give up WebSurveyor, the idea of securing my financial future after living so close to the edge financially was really appealing. We ultimately sold the company to a private equity firm.

Though I didn't get the wealth influx that some at that time did, I was able to cash out with enough to secure my family's immediate future and give me tremendous flexibility for what I wanted to do with the next chapter of my life.

By 2007, I felt I had arrived. I was in my mid-forties, Jocelyn was heading off to college (which was now paid for), Davey and Julia were happy and healthy, Allison had been teaching at the high school our kids attended, and we could afford to go on some really nice vacations with our extended family.

I took some time off, focusing on getting my body healthy after a decade of stress from being an entrepreneur and a highly engaged parent. Between working out daily, cycling hundreds of miles a week, and running regularly, I was in the best shape of my life.

Before long I jumped back into start-up life and spun up a series of product/service ideas—some moderately successful, some simply expensive learning experiences. I still felt the need to build up another business, though, and the idea that I could possibly get my kids involved in it had tremendous appeal now that they were each on the verge of becoming an independent adult.

Riding the Waves

July 25, 2016

The grief I was experiencing came in waves.

I would sit in a daze, pretending to go through the motions of life, and suddenly a thought would drop into my active consciousness. *Why did this happen? Is Davey really gone? Why didn't I do something that could have prevented this? I want to go back in time and fix this!*

These thoughts were the ones that always seemed to activate a wave. The pull of grief would begin and before I knew it, it would come crashing down on my head, causing a fit of pain that radiated from my heart and seemed to hit every part of my body. Sometimes it would be brief, sometimes long, but the only thing that seemed to alleviate it was crying, and sometimes screaming out when I was completely alone. My body was physically manifesting the grief that needed to be released and crying was the only way to do it.

Once the fit of crying subsided, I would feel relieved, but far from normal. The pain would be replaced by a dazed feeling, a disorientation; my life was completely changed.

This cycle would then repeat, though thankfully the waves became a little further apart each time.

My carefully crafted life was in ruins. Everything I prided myself on felt damaged. My wife and daughters seemed inconsolably sad. My close friends and family now treated me completely differently; warm smiles and happy greetings were replaced with looks of pity and cautious queries about how I was holding up. The business I had been working on felt pointless now.

I felt as though every single thought I had before the accident was packaged up in a small container and placed on a shelf in front of me. I could see all of them sitting there, waiting for me to snap off the lid and load them back into my head, but I just couldn't seem to get the boxes open.

It was the beginning of my realization that while I couldn't control all of the thoughts that ran through my brain, I could decide which of them I wanted to engage.

The Family Business

January 29, 2016

"Dad, what do think if I joined you and Jocelyn in the business?"

It was the end of January 2016 and Davey had graduated the month before from James Madison University with a BS in Economics. He had no idea what he wanted to do next, and earlier in the month he had announced that he was moving to Southern California, where most of our family still lived.

But after a few weeks of looking for jobs in the L.A. area from afar, he was starting to get restless. All his friends from high school and college had jobs in the DC area. He was hanging out with them and enjoying himself so much that he decided maybe living in DC wouldn't be that bad after all.

Jocelyn and I had started working on a concept for a business about four months earlier. It was a software product that helped teach people to be safer online, from a security standpoint. Though Jocelyn had a full-time job already and lived in DC with her boyfriend, she would call, or we would meet in person to work on our idea. As a longtime entrepreneur myself, I had always been excited by the prospect of having a family business.

The product we were building needed a fairly large amount of content—a job that would be perfect for Davey. We worked out a plan where our little start-up would pay Davey a nominal salary every week, and he would work on the project full time and focus on building up the content we needed.

I work from home and have a decent-size office, so we went out and bought a desk and office chair for Davey and set it up right across from my work space. We hung a couple of whiteboards so we could brainstorm ideas, and before long our little office was up and running. Jocelyn would contribute when she could, coming into our office or video conferencing in as we rapidly progressed the product.

Though the first couple of months went a little slowly, getting to work with my kids was a dream come true for me. By mid April 2016 we had hit our stride and the application was coming along really well. A month later I started showing a very early alpha stage to prospective customers and the feedback was encouraging.

Davey accompanied me on some of the meetings I had with potential customers. It was a wonderful feeling to watch him grow into the young man I had always anticipated him becoming. I would occasionally overhear Davey talking to one of his friends about the business and how much he enjoyed being an entrepreneur. It was tremendously gratifying as his dad!

When summer officially arrived and Allison was done with school, she packed up and headed to our summer home in Bethany Beach, Delaware. This was her summer routine — Allison and one or more of the kids would spend that time at the beach and I would commute the three hours there on the weekends. Since Julia was still in college she had the summer off and worked there full time. Jocelyn had long since moved out on her own, which left Davey and me working from our home in Virginia.

On the weekdays I was in Virginia I would talk to Allison on the phone every night. We'd catch up quickly and inevitably I'd tell Allison how incredibly happy I was getting to work with the kids every day. I didn't take it for granted, that's for sure. I was tremendously appreciative of everything I had.

Davey and I had a nice routine. I was the early riser, getting into our office at the crack of dawn. Davey would come in an hour or so later. We each broke up the day by going out to lunch or getting some exercise outside. By late afternoon Davey would be out on the driveway, shooting hoops and coaxing me into a little one-on-one game of basketball.

I came close to beating him only once. He wrapped up his backyard basketball career against me with a perfect undefeated record.

Changing Course

"Life is what happens to you while you are busy making other plans."
—John Lennon, "Beautiful Boy (Darling Boy)"

The three days leading up to Davey's accident are permanently etched into my mind. It was a Monday morning in the middle of July—hot and muggy even by Virginia standards—when Davey came down into our shared office after his morning run. He sat down and looked at me, then suddenly burst into tears. I was more than a little shocked and asked him what was wrong.

Monday, July 18, 2016
"I finally believe in God. I mean, I really believe, and it feels amazing!"

We spent the morning talking about God and the universe. I shared with Davey my thoughts of how it all worked. He was extremely interested in my perspective, which at that point wasn't very well defined. I hedged quite a bit, because I didn't have a "belief system" per se. I was well versed, however, in a series of different concepts that ranged from my traditional Catholic upbringing to some of the more science-based perspectives I had read and understood. I didn't feel strongly about any of it, though—they were just data points for me.

As an engineer, I tend to look at things as objectively as possible. I understood and could deeply appreciate the teachings of Jesus, but the inconsistencies in the Bible, the sometimes violent history of the church, and my appreciation for how science helped explain the universe in an evidence-based way left me…agnostic.

Davey, however, kept saying that he just suddenly believed and knew. He couldn't really describe how or why; instead he would change the focus of our conversations to ask what I thought and believed.

Then he said something that I didn't expect to hear from him:

"Dad, you're my soul mate."

I'd never heard anyone reference a soul mate in any context other than lovers in a relationship. To hear this from my son was both a little odd and one of the most loving things he could have said to me. Allison would later tell me that Davey said the same thing to her the next day: "Mom, you're my soul mate. You just get me."

As we talked through the morning, Davey hung on my every word—he seemed deeply interested in what I had to say. After a while I tried to steer the conversation back to work and Davey changed gears, telling me that he may have a girlfriend.

My initial reaction of concern changed a bit—he was in love!

After a few hours of discussion, I became adamant that we start focusing on work. While I was optimistic about our start-up, the tough part of getting the product finalized before launch was starting to gnaw at me—and even that was just the beginning of building a successful business around it.

Both of us dropped back into "heads down" mode and worked through our respective lists of tasks for the rest of the day.

In the evening, I reengaged Davey over dinner. I grilled some steaks for us and we each had a glass of wine as he told me a little more about his girlfriend. She was from New Jersey, attended James Madison University with him, and had just moved to Arlington. He said that they had dated on and off but had not been ready to meet each other's parents—but Davey was now ready to do that. We talked about relationships a bit and my son seemed genuinely happy.

Tuesday – July 19, 2016
The next morning seemed to start out as usual, though very early for Davey. I left the house at 6 a.m. for a run, the same three-mile route that Davey always ran. I had heard him head out of the house earlier in the morning, which was surprising.

About a half-mile into my run I saw Davey ahead of me, running in my direction, on the final leg of his run. When we were about fifty yards apart I could see his big grin and he immediately started to sprint toward me as though completing a race. As he got close he put up his hand and high-fived me as he went by, making me smile and laugh.

Later that morning we were both in the office and I started talking to Davey about considering a slightly different approach to our product launch. He seemed engaged as discussed what our focus should be. Davey wrote quite a few notes on his whiteboard and then began jamming away on his MacBook, while listening to music through his headphones.

At one point in the morning Davey looked up from his work and told me that over the weekend he had encountered a woman while he was refueling his car. She was approaching each person at the pumps and asking for money, telling each that her car was out of gas and she needed money. He ignored her request, finished refueling, and got in to drive away. But something told him to stop and as he was pulling his car out of the gas station he called the woman over and gave her the $15 in change left over from paying for his gas.

As he explained this story to me he said he realized she needed the money more than he did, even though Davey had very little money himself. "She's a person and I felt like everyone was ignoring her," he said. I told Davey how proud I was of him, that his kindness was a wonderful attribute.

By mid-afternoon, though, things started to get a little...odd. Davey said he was going to work out back, next to our pool. He had his MacBook out there with him and was at least putting on the appearance of working. But I went out several times to talk to him and he didn't seem to be doing any of our start-up work. He appeared to be listening to music on his Mac and reading something online, though I couldn't tell what.

Sitting down next to him, I told him we really needed to focus if we wanted this business to be successful. I was trying to motivate him and get him to start focusing on work. But he seemed completely uninterested. I started to get very concerned.

"Dad, you're too focused on money," he said. "You should focus on love. Love is everything."

He seemed to be in a completely different state of mind than he had been just a few hours earlier. I returned to my office, deeply worried that maybe he was on something.

We talked again at dinner and things continued to go in a direction that made me anxious. He told me that he needed to figure out what he wanted to do and that while he loved me and wanted to live in the area, he didn't want to work on our start-up anymore. He said he didn't want to be part of the rat race, though he wasn't sure what he wanted to do now. We went back and forth a lot. It ended on a rather sad note, with him saying he was done working with me, but that he would be fine.

To say that I was massively disappointed would be an understatement. I loved working with Davey, and to hear him say he didn't want to be involved in the business anymore left me shocked and frustrated. I was also now going to have to determine how our business—already in a precarious state at this stage—would even survive.

I tried to talk through his line of thinking with him and see if I could get him to come back around. He had been so excited about our work just the previous Friday—it didn't make sense. I began to again wonder if he had taken something. A drug maybe? Some medication that was affecting his judgment?

Allison was always my sounding board, so I tried reaching her by phone, but she didn't answer. I left multiple messages asking her to call me back but she never did. Later that evening Julia told me Allison had been out on a dock at the beach, walked backward while having her picture taken, and fell into the water, destroying her phone, which was in her purse. That was why I couldn't reach her.

I was on my own.

Wednesday – July 20, 2016
I woke up the next morning at 5 a.m. to what I thought was yelling outside. I peered out our bedroom window and saw Davey pacing around the pool in the predawn light.

He had his headphones in and at first I thought he was singing. I cracked open the window and I heard him saying really loudly, "God, how do I hear you?"

I slipped on some clothes and went out into the backyard to talk to him. He didn't notice me at first. He was now running back and forth on the lawn at full speed. It seemed like he had so much energy in his body that he just couldn't contain it.

When he finally noticed me standing there he seemed surprised. We talked for just a few moments; I told him I was worried about him and he told me I just didn't understand, that he was so incredibly happy and that he was fine.

He went out for what I thought was his usual run, but it turned out he was running all the way to a local park, a difficult three-and-a-half-mile path down a winding road with no sidewalk.

I finally spoke to Allison and told her that I was really worried about Davey and thought maybe he had been taking something, because he seemed so different. Between his behavior and my worry about the business, I felt like I was in free fall. For a person like me who needs to be in control, this was incredibly uncomfortable.

Allison said she would call him. I tried to get some work done, but it was impossible for me to focus. I had this intense feeling of dread that I couldn't shake. I spoke to Jocelyn and shared my concerns about Davey and she said she would leave for our house as soon as she could from DC.

Soon after, both Allison and Julia spoke to him on the phone, and then Allison called me. She told me not to worry, that Davey had just found God and that everything was OK. He was in love with a girl and was genuinely happy.

Then Davey called me. He said, "Dad, what's wrong? Are you okay? Mom is worried about you!" I broke down and started crying. The stress of Davey behaving so oddly was really worrying me and I couldn't shake the incredible feeling of dread building up in me.

I told him that I'd been working so hard on everything and that the stress was too much. That I loved him and that I was worried about him. Davey tried to keep me on the phone and told me that he was heading back home as fast as he could.

After I hung up, I went out to our screened-in porch and sat down on a chair, staring out at our wooded backyard. I was in that chair when Davey came outside to me. He leaned over my shoulder and gave me this tremendous hug, pushing the side of his face against mine. I started to sob—I was an emotional wreck at this point. Davey kept repeating, "It's okay, Dad, I'm right here. I'll never leave you! I will always be with you!"—he must have said it two or three times. After a while he settled into the couch across from me.

He said, "Dad, it's okay. I'm fine!" And he did look fine, all of a sudden. He had his usual bright smile and he looked really happy. He told me that he realized that he had thrown my entire world upside down and that he would work on the business for a little longer to help out.

Then he went out to the backyard to listen to music and read on his MacBook.

With all that was going on with Davey, I asked Allison to make the three-hour drive home from the beach as quickly as possible. Though she didn't have the same sense of dread I did, she realized that I needed help managing all of this. I think she was more worried about me than she was about Davey. As we were having a large dead tree removed from front yard of our beach house, it would take Allison a few hours to wrap everything up before she could leave. In retrospect, there were several extraordinary obstacles placed in Allison's path that prevented her from getting home quickly.

Jocelyn finally arrived, and talked at length to Davey. Afterward, she came in, while Davey stayed in the backyard by the pool. She shared my concern for his state of mind. He was out back pacing around the pool, again with that restless energy.

Back in my office for a conference call, I looked up to see Davey walk by the office door toward the garage. I glanced over at his desk and noticed his wallet sitting there. I figured he was probably going to shoot some hoops in the backyard.

Instead he went out to his car, telling Jocelyn he was heading to River Bend Park to go for a run.

The accident happened about ten minutes later. According to the witness that was driving the other way, they saw Davey's car heading toward them, straddling the double yellow line on a narrow, curving part of the road. They said he appeared to be looking down at something, likely his phone, and that when he looked up and saw the approaching car he swerved and over-corrected.

He missed the oncoming car but lost control of his own and struck the tree. He died instantly.

At least that was what I was told. I would soon learn that Davey wasn't really dead.

Awakening

As a parent you spend a lifetime helping your children navigate through new phases in life. For my children I was there, checking out new schools, or bringing them to new sports they wanted to try out, or escorting them to new friends' houses to meet the parents. As they got older I went to visit college campuses or help them move into new housing.

As weird as it may sound, I desperately wanted to know what had happened to my son once he preceded me into the afterlife. What happens after physical death had been an abstract concept to me up to this point in my life. Though I had lost my mother five years earlier, she was in her eighties and her health had been in decline for years. It was…expected. I had been mentally preparing for my mother's passing for over a year, yet it was still very difficult losing her.

Davey's passing happened so quickly and he was so young — so I was in shock as well as grief. Was that it? Was Davey really gone? His physical body had ceased functioning but I couldn't shake the feeling that he was still around me.

By the Tuesday after Davey's accident most of our family had left and my brother, Daryl was the last to make the long flight back home. He graciously offered to take on the most difficult jobs that came up after Davey's accident. The last thing I wanted was to have the memory of my son's body lying on the cold steel gurney of a morgue burned in my head — my brother offered to go to the funeral home that held his body and identify his remains, a requirement prior to the cremation we had requested.

In addition, my brother went to the auto-wrecking yard to retrieve Davey's personal possessions from his car. Since Daryl was a former deputy sheriff, he had seen more than his share of accidents and felt he would be better equipped to handle this process. He returned from that task confirming that it was better we didn't see his car because the damage had been so extensive.

Daryl was always spiritually oriented, fascinated by the paranormal and sensitive to things that most people overlooked. He wanted to know the details of the days leading up to Davey's accident, and talked to Jocelyn, Julia, Allison, and me about it. Each of us shared the recent conversations we'd had with Davey.

Daryl and I sat down in our screened-in porch the day before he was to fly back to California. I was completely conflicted, alternating between feeling Davey's presence and questioning how this could possibly happen. Daryl played sheriff's deputy and asked me again to recount all that had happened in the days leading up to Davey's accident—from his sudden belief in God to the many conversations we had, including on the day of the accident, when Davey hugged me and said "I will never leave you." I was so completely consumed with my grief and in such a state of shock that I struggled to put it all together.

Daryl asked, "Have you considered that these events were part of the divine? That this was part of a plan? It sounds like Davey knew what was happening."

Davey wasn't perfect, but he was as close to perfect as a human could get in my eyes, even if my analytical brain accounted for fatherly bias. When others gossiped about someone, Davey would never jump in. He had a childlike wonder about nature and would look at the wildlife in our

49

backyard with awe and reverence. He had an easy laugh and a bright smile that lit up the room. If there was ever a hugging contest, Davey would be the hands-down winner—when he embraced you, you immediately felt connected to him.

When Daryl suggested that this may have been a divine event, it triggered something in me. All I had to dwell on up to this point were small fragments of what had just happened. Laying them out sequentially and looking at them from a detached standpoint, as my brother was doing, made me think maybe there was more to this than I'd originally considered. Was there a larger plan at work? Was there a divine purpose to what was happening to us?

The left side of my brain—the analytical engineer in me—immediately concluded that a celestial entity coming up with a plan to kill my son was not something I would entertain. It made no logical sense.

The right side of my brain—the creative side that was open and becoming more aware—was intrigued. The ever-present grief regained control quickly, though, and pushed these thoughts into the background.

Fleeting Joy

Daryl was the last to head back home. Allison and Julia then left to return to Bethany Beach, where Julia had long-standing plans to celebrate her twenty-first birthday, though none of us had any idea how that could possibly go on.

I was home alone for the first time since the accident, though I would be heading out to Bethany later that day to be with Allison and Julia.

I lingered in my home office, sitting at my desk and working through some important emails and business tasks before heading out. I sat in my chair and stared across the room at Davey's empty desk. His laptop, chair, headphones, books, and notes were all unmoved since the day of the accident. His whiteboard still had the to-do list he had written just a week earlier about our business, a list I could not even consider.

My grief was still intense and I had a very hard time focusing on anything other than how much I missed my son. How would I ever be able to carry on without him? I packed up my things and headed out on the three-hour drive to Bethany Beach. Throughout that long drive I was deeply sad, and I kept talking to Davey while I drove. More than a few tears were shed.

I love you, buddy.
I miss you so much.

This became my mantra as I drove, repeating it over and over again.

While passing a cornfield in Delaware, I had a profound experience. It started as this warm feeling that radiated from my heart and quickly enveloped my entire body. I can only describe the feeling as intense joy. It pushed every aspect of the pain and grief I had been experiencing out of my body and replaced it with a sense of happiness and love.

I found myself enveloped in pure contentment. I knew in that moment that everything was going to be okay. Slowly, the feeling subsided, but the grief didn't return immediately.

I spent the next five days at the beach, trying as much as possible to reconstruct my life. The restaurant Julia worked at — Mango's — organized a paddle out in Davey's honor. A ritual practiced in many surfing communities around the world, a paddle out is a celebration of the life of a surfer that has passed and we felt honored that our community organized it. The local surf shop brought dozens of surfboards for everyone and many of Davey's high school and college friends made the long trek out to the beach to honor their friend.

Davey loved to surf and was very good at it. He and his best friend, Spencer Brookbank, would often go out early to catch waves before working their summer jobs at the beach. On days when the waves weren't great Davey would just sit out on his board, staring out at the ocean. He truly loved being in the water.

Over forty of us jumped on surfboards and paddled out beyond the small waves, each with flowers clamped in our mouths. We formed a circle, said a few words about Davey, and I thanked everyone for supporting us. We all threw our flowers into the middle of the circle and then splashed and yelled out in joy — it was a tremendously moving experience.

Someone would later send me a picture that was taken from the shore. The circle we made was just beginning to form and there were some high clouds as the sun lit up our group. The photo captured shafts of sunlight beaming down on us.

When I look at that photo I picture Davey sitting on his board just beyond our little circle, facing out to the vast ocean and waiting for that perfect wave.

Talking to Davey

I stayed with Allison and Julia at the beach for a week before heading back to Virginia. My old habits took over and I felt the need to get moving again, to get my business started back up after suffering such an extraordinary loss. Not only had I lost my only son, I had also lost one of the co-founders of my business.

Being home alone, whether it was sitting at my desk and staring at Davey's empty chair or walking in our backyard amongst the birds and butterflies around me, the grief was an ever-present companion.

I began talking to Davey, sometimes just quietly in my head and other times out loud. On one Monday, I just couldn't get myself motivated to do actual work. I sat down at my computer and decided to write a letter to Davey.

I stared at the blank screen and blinking cursor, unsure of what I wanted to say. How do you address a letter to someone that is dead? Instead I wrote the first thing that came to my mind.

I don't know if I can do this.

To my surprise, after every sentence I wrote I heard an immediate response from Davey in my head. I recorded that as well. When I wrote my words to Davey they came out hesitatingly, because I was forming them as I typed and was in deep pain as I wrote them, but when I "heard" Davey's response the words came through so quickly I had difficulty keeping up. The fully formed response was just there, waiting for me to type it out.

I don't know if I can do this.

You can, Dad, it's okay. I'm right here.

I just miss you so much, buddy. These waves of grief are just so intense, sometimes I feel like I'm being pulled into a black hole.

I know it hurts but you have to remember that I'm right here with you! Right now as you are typing this. These are my words, not yours.

I just don't know how I'm going to be able to live a normal, happy life again. This all feels so hopeless right now.

It's NOT hopeless. You wouldn't believe how wonderful God is, how beautiful where I am now is. I know you are struggling right now, but where I am time doesn't exist. You're already here. I am surrounded by unconditional love. I'm with our entire family all the time.

You have no idea how much I want to believe that.

I do know how much you want to believe that.

I want to be there now—I want to be surrounded by unconditional love and be free of pain now.

What you don't realize is that you already are.

What do you mean? How can I be? I hurt so much right now.

You are letting your physical body feel pain. But you can control it, you just need to learn how. Remember when I came to you on Monday and told you that I finally got it? That I believed in God?

Of course, I can't stop thinking about those three days leading up to your accident.

It was God telling me that my time in the physical world had been completed. I had experienced the life I was meant to live and that it was time for me to return to God. It's really hard to describe, Dad—words don't work too well for this, at least not in a way that you will really understand.

I want to believe that so badly.

But you do believe it!

I don't understand. How can I believe it if I don't?

Beliefs change over time. You have changed your belief system over time based on things that have happened to you, right?

Yes.

Time is something that only exists in the physical world. When you think of eternity you think "a really long time," but that's not how eternity works. Eternity isn't a line that runs forever; it just doesn't really exist at all. Eternity doesn't "start" and "stop," it just is.

You may not fully believe what I'm telling you at your point in time but here, where I am, you do believe. In your physical existence it will just take time for you to really understand and believe it. There's a reason they call it faith.

So can I just skip ahead and be there now? Why do I have to experience this pain?

It's not your time yet! You still have a life to experience before you are back here. Mom and Jocelyn and Julia need you! You have more to do, more to experience. Some of it will be really hard but most of it will be wonderful and beautiful. You just need to understand that you can control how you react to that physical world you are in.

Stop thinking that all you have is this physical existence and that defines who you are. While you are living that physical existence you are also here with God. You felt it a couple of times since I left. That peaceful feeling that washed over you and made you feel happy and content.

I loved that feeling. I want it back but I don't know how to make it happen. It just...happened.

Right now you are focused on my physical loss. Even though I can talk to you, that physical sadness is still there. But you can control it. You just need to focus on the positive energy that flows through you. Let go of that sadness that you keep visiting. You really don't need to do that. You are not honoring my memory, or demonstrating to me how much you loved me.

The love you have for me is eternal too! You don't need to "remember" it, that love will always be there.

I'm constantly looking out in the backyard, at the butterflies and the birds. I keep repeating that "I love you, buddy," but it just seems to make me feel the loss even more.

Do you really think you are going to forget me? That I need to be told that you love me so that I will stay with you? I'm a part of you, just as you were a part of me, and I don't mean in that physical DNA sense. You don't need to do that. There is an entire physical world that you are in right now. It is beautiful and wonderful and God created it so that you can experience life. Focus on the life you have in front of you!

But I miss you so much. I miss seeing you in the morning, or playing those one-on-one basketball games where you kicked my butt. I miss seeing you when I was going for my morning run.

You got to experience those times though, right?

Yes, of course. I'll always treasure those memories.

That's just how life works. We get to experience things. Some make us feel good, some don't. But in the physical world they start and then they stop. The physical world has time limits. You aren't meant to live out the physical world doing the same thing over and over again. The physical world is about change. God created the physical world and let it run to see that change. Your purpose is to experience life! To feel all of it. To learn and absorb as much as you can. You need to focus on that.

I will try, buddy. Thank you.

You know all that you need to know, it's just hidden under all of the baggage that comes with physical existence. There is one thing that will get you through this: love.

I love you, buddy.

I love you too! And know that I will never leave you. I'm always there with you.

I pushed my chair back from my desk and stared at the words I had just written. *Did that really just happen?*

Some of what Davey told me in that conversation didn't make sense to me. It wasn't until later, when I started to read books about the afterlife and spirituality, that I would see a tremendous similarity to what Davey was describing.

I reread our conversation half a dozen times that day, marveling at the thought that I had just spoken to my son. This didn't feel like wishful thinking or some kind of coping mechanism, it felt like an actual conversation.

Connections

We noticed immediately after Davey's passing that we were connecting to other people in ways we didn't expect. A friend gave us a book written by Lee Ann Evans called *Believing Is Seeing*, which she wrote after her daughter Katelyn passed in an automobile accident; like Davey she was driving solo, the car struck a tree, and she died instantly.

Allison read her book and immediately gave it to me, insisting I read it. As I turned the pages I recognized many similarities in our journey to what the author was experiencing. When I hit the middle of the book I found it contained a selection of photos of Lee Ann, Katelyn, and her family.

I suddenly realized that I knew one of the people in her family! Lee Ann's brother, Kelly and I had worked together fifteen years earlier. It seemed so odd that I would find a picture of a former co-worker in the middle of a book I was reading. It also turned out that Lee Ann lived in Burke, Virginia, not far from our home.

Lately I had been hearing "watch out for the signs," which seemed initially like an attempt to make anything that happened fit the narrative that it was a sign from the spirit world trying to get my attention. The skeptic in me dismissed it as such, but a growing part of my mind started to accept that receiving *Believing Is Seeing* was actually a sign from my son that we needed to make contact with Lee Ann.

I reached out to Lee Ann on Facebook and she connected with me. Within a few weeks she was visiting us at our home and a wonderful friendship started between her family and ours.

Reading Lee Ann's book led me to others, especially those that dealt with spiritual perspectives on death and the survival of consciousness. I couldn't seem to consume enough information about life after death and actively sought out books that would help me better understand these concepts. What I found was a tremendous consistency from a wide range of sources.

Lee Ann brought us a copy of *Growing Up in Heaven* by James Van Praagh, a very well known psychic medium who has written many books on the connections he has helped people make with their loved ones in the afterlife. This particular book was aimed toward parents that had lost a child, whether young children or adult children. The book was like a lifeline and deeply resonated with me.

My concept of the afterlife at that point was based on the Bible and traditional Catholic teachings, which I often struggled with throughout my life. The belief system I had been handed in my youth could be summed up as follows: you get one shot at physical life, it begins at birth, you live your life according to the rules approved by the church, and at the end of your life you're judged by God and either gained access to heaven, go off to purgatory for some time and then get in, or spend eternal damnation in hell. Or at least those were the salient points as I saw them.

I want to stop here and note that I don't judge anyone for their belief system. If you are a devout Catholic and the teachings of the church resonate with you, then I'm genuinely happy for you. Your view of the church may be very different than mine. Having been raised in a Catholic household (and attending Catholic schools up until high school), I never felt a deep connection to the religion or the church. The priests that conducted mass and the teachers at our school always seemed to emphasize what would happen to me if I didn't obey. While they also emphasized love and kindness, there was always that veiled threat that if I didn't do what I was told there would literally be hell to pay.

I respect an individual's innate right to believe whatever feels right to them, and that includes atheism. I have always felt strongly that you are the only one that can believe something—it cannot be handed to you by someone who insists you believe it. You either do or you don't. A belief system is the one thing that is authentically yours and if you become a surrogate for the beliefs of others, without being able to question those beliefs, then you are not being true to yourself.

My beliefs have changed over time, as new evidence or concepts are presented to me, and I try to process them as rationally as I can. At this point in my life—less than a month after losing Davey—I was still desperately seeking answers to fundamental questions that up until then had simply not been all that important to me. This was all very new territory for me.

Van Praagh's book put the conversations I had with Davey in the days leading up to his accident into a new light and helped open my eyes to a different perspective—that life not only doesn't end with death, it also doesn't begin with birth. While I was familiar with the concept of reincarnation, I was highly skeptical of it and never gave it any deep thought. Van Praagh presented the idea of life being a school for eternal souls to learn within human limits, and that certainly sounded interesting.

So much of what I was reading matched up with what I heard from Davey the day I "channeled" him; I use quotes because it was a new term for me, something I wasn't even sure was real at the time.

The skeptic in me would often chime in at this point, with doubts that any of this was true. One moment I would be overjoyed to consider a continuation of consciousness beyond physical life, and the next my thoughts would cast doubts about all of it and dismiss it all as physical reactions to grief.

At this point all I really wanted was to be normal again, but I was really struggling with what that meant.

Davey's Gift

In the immediate aftermath of Davey's accident we found that people wanted to express their sympathy by sending us flowers. While this may appeal to some folks, Allison and I both found it not only unnecessary but difficult to process. Having just lost our son, the last thing we wanted was dozens of vases of flowers around our house that needed attention and would quickly be in a state of decay themselves.

Instead, Allison got the idea that what she wanted was a web presence, where we could ask people to perform some act of kindness in Davey's honor and record it for everyone to see. Davey was always helping other people and now that gap needed to be filled.

Julia quickly put together a Facebook page, Davey's Gift, to collect these acts of kindness, asking people to do something nice, then look up to the sky and say "That's for you, Davey." Within a few days entries of wonderful gestures began pouring in, initially from around our community but quickly from different parts of the country and then all over the world. People that had never met Davey (maybe he was a friend of a friend) were inspired to do a kind act in his name and did so, recording it for us.

Some of the stories were incredibly touching. We found ourselves looking forward every day to reading the amazing things people had done in our son's name. Providing a meal for a homeless person, donating blood, collecting books for a military hospital, providing school supplies for homeless children...there were hundreds of entries and each helped lighten the load of grief we were carrying, knowing that Davey's name was associated with these gestures.

Many acts of kindness came with beautiful stories of the impact they had provided. One friend bought a young person an unlimited monthly subway pass in New York when she saw him asking for a quick swipe to get to the next station. As she gave him the pass and explained the story behind Davey's Acts of Kindness, the young man got a strange look on his face and asked if he could borrow her cell phone. He made a quick call and returned her phone, telling her that he had run away from home weeks before over a trivial argument and had been living in the subway station this entire time. Her act of kindness had given him the courage to return home.

Another friend related how he bought a bunch of smoothies at a grocery store on a hot summer day, and as he walked out to give them away, the first man he offered one gratefully accepted. When our friend explained the reason behind it, the man became choked up. He said he had just lost his brother the week before and he really needed that gesture.

A teacher named Jo Hensel in Northern California, the mother of one of my co-workers from years ago, decided to make Davey's Acts of Kindness her class activity for the year. Each of her students would perform regular acts of kindness and Jo would record them on the Facebook page. This led to our family connecting with those students and experiencing a beautiful relationship with an entire middle school class. We sent them the glow in the dark wrist bands we all wore to remember Davey, they sent us beautiful cards and letters, and it kicked off relationship that continue to this day.

There was something beautiful in asking people to do this. Each person had effectively become an extension of our son. They were helping Davey perform an entire lifetime of kindness. The joy it provided us was immeasurable.

Family

We were always very close to our extended family, even after we moved from California to Virginia over two decades earlier. At least a couple times a year we would get together for large vacations, and it was always an opportunity to reconnect and have fun, whether it was just sitting around a house or on an elaborate destination vacation. Allison's parents had remained very active as they got older and continued to be a part of our adventures.

Since the bulk of the extended family would go on these vacations, they needed to be planned far in advance — buying plane tickets, making hotel reservations, etc. nearly a year ahead of time. When Davey's accident happened we had three major events booked: we were hosting a family reunion just six weeks later at our home and we had two international destinations planned: a tropical Christmas vacation and a wedding in Mexico for a close friend of the family.

With the reunion just around the corner and the flights booked, we decided to press ahead and get everyone together for the long Labor Day weekend. Instead of it being a reunion, we turned it into another opportunity to celebrate Davey and perform acts of kindness in his name. We all drove into Washington, DC, and visited the National Mall, handing out bottled water to the adults and small toys to every child we came across.

It was interesting, because as we did this people were very defensive at first. Washington, DC, is a place where one is often accosted by people asking for money, to sign a petition or market some new energy drink, so it was understandable. As soon as we explained that there were no strings attached, that we were just doing acts of kindness in honor of our son, people became not just appreciative but incredibly compassionate. Many handshakes and hugs were exchanged and we all walked away from the experience better for it.

Having the extended family there was still bittersweet at this point. There is nothing that brings home how fragile life is than seeing a loss so close up, and it was clear that each parent in the family was hugging their own kids a little tighter. Seeing that was hard at first, my own loss coming to the forefront of my mind whenever any parental affection was demonstrated. This wasn't the fault of anyone — and in fact it would have been odd if they hadn't done that — but it was just another part of getting through the grief that I had to learn how to manage.

At the end of the year it was time for our tropical vacation over the Christmas holiday, and we all headed off to an all-inclusive resort in the Dominican Republic. One result of having all adult children was that drinking had become a major component of our vacations, and days were often spent sitting by a pool or beach with many family members, drinking large amounts of alcohol.

Since Davey's passing I had not drunk much alcohol. I was never much of a drinker — mostly because I had seen what it did to my dad — and the drinking I did do was limited to social occasions. At this point, we were five months into processing our grief and I had started to feel like I was getting a handle on it, so I indulged in tropical drinks and beer nearly every day. It didn't take long to realize that when I got enough alcohol in me, the filters that kept negative thoughts out of my head disappeared and suddenly I was deep in the throes of grief again. I learned the hard way to dramatically limit my alcohol consumption.

While I was able to talk openly to our family members about Davey and some of the more mystical experiences I'd had, the women seemed to have more interest in sharing their thoughts and hearing what I had been learning. Meditation was something I had just started to use as a way of connecting with Davey, and my nieces and daughters were very interested in learning more, even sitting down and trying meditation with me. If you had told me a year earlier that by the following Christmas I would be sitting in lotus position on a beach, doing meditation exercises with my daughters and nieces instead of floating in the pool with a drink in my hand, I would have laughed at you!

The last remaining vacation we had that Davey had been planning to attend was the wedding of family friends Caitlyn and Matt in Mexico. This was a huge event and our daughter Jocelyn was one of the bridesmaids. Being with the family for such a wonderful occasion was excellent and since I had learned to significantly limit my alcohol intake I was able to have a really good time.

The wedding itself was one of the prettiest I had ever seen; the old hacienda that hosted it had beautiful grounds and the weather was perfect. The night of the wedding culminated in a large outdoor reception complete with fireworks to celebrate the event. We were all just in awe.

But as the bride and groom had their first dance together as husband and wife, I thought about Davey and sadness started to grip me, knowing that I would never see him get married or have that first dance. When I looked at my own bride sitting next to me I could see the tears starting to come down her face, and I knew this was having a big impact on her too.

I put my arm around her shoulders and tried my best to comfort her. Next, the father of the bride and the mother of the groom came out and started to dance with their children, and that triggered intense pain for Allison, knowing that she would not get to have that experience with her son. She quickly got up and left, going to the bathroom to compose herself so as not to put a damper on what was otherwise a beautiful and loving moment. She insisted that I stay at the table as she got up.

Her sister Jeanne, our niece Joyce, and our daughter Julia quickly got up and went to her aid, joining her in the bathroom and giving her comfort. My brother-in-law Gary moved over next to me as he saw me struggling to maintain my own composure and put his arm around my shoulders.

Gary and I had been in the same family for over thirty years and we had been through a lot together. I always felt close to Gary, and since Davey's passing I had seen a change in him too. He was always very close to our son and this loss had a huge impact on him. He seemed to sense the pain I was experiencing and was making regular efforts to be there for me.

Since we had both married into the extended family, we often referred to ourselves as brother-out-laws; that changed after all this happened. He became more like a true brother and I deeply appreciated it.

Our entire family was pulling together, the grief hitting each of us differently. The healing for each of us came at a different pace but slowly we were all getting back to a new normal that was even more loving than it had been before. Many of the petty competitions became irrelevant, the arguments about politics pointless. There was now a depth to how each of us expressed love to one another.

Reintegrating

It took me a while to learn to talk to people outside of my immediate friends and family. The first few weeks were clearly the hardest because of people wanting to demonstrate how sorry they were. I felt like an exhibit at the Zoo of Sorrow; people would come to visit but there was a barrier between me and them. I could hear laughter and sense people having a good time outside of my little cage and I desperately wanted to join them.

When I first started to leave the comfortable confines of our home, I learned something interesting. I desperately wanted to talk about my son, since Davey was still very much the primary topic on my mind.

In my first few light conversations with strangers after the accident I found myself quickly blurting out that my son had recently passed, often with barely any transition in the discussion. I had become like an awkward teenager trying to talk to the opposite sex, but instead of hormones clouding my thought processes it was the grief. I was clearly not my usual self and I think I was just trying to justify it, even with strangers that likely didn't know anything was wrong.

I learned rather quickly that bringing up the loss of a child was the best way to blow a hole into the middle of any budding conversation. It would either be quickly terminated with an "I'm so sorry" or "I can't imagine," or it would veer into a strange place, with well intentioned people telling me how they had lost an aging grandparent and knew exactly how I felt.

My ego would take over in those instances and insist that my grief was so much worse than theirs. How could they even begin to know what I was going through? I would keep those thoughts to myself in the moment, but I would bottle them up and replay them later, adding anger to the grief I felt—which was not healthy for me. It didn't take long for me to realize that if I wanted to talk to people and share anything about myself it was best for now if I didn't bring up my son's passing.

A cab ride from the airport resulted in a nice conversation between the driver and me. It started with pleasantries about each of our days and the weather, just some surface-level things that came up easily. He told me about his kids and his hopes for them in the USA; he was an immigrant and wanted a better life for them. Clearly the man had taken on some significant challenges in order to provide for his family and I found myself deeply admiring him.

After about ten minutes of chatting he asked if I had any children.

My mind went on high alert—do I tell him? I felt I was connecting with him and didn't want to crush the conversation, since I was enjoying it so much. But the last thing I wanted to do was deny that I had a son. Davey was still my boy and I still felt completely connected to him.

"Yes, I have three adult children. Two girls and a boy."

He said he had a son as well and his was still in high school, trying to figure out where he would go to college and what he should major in. He asked what my son did for a living.

"He's been working on a start-up with me. It's a computer security product."

While I was able to say this to him and sound normal, underneath my exterior shell I was feeling a wave of grief begin to form. I quickly began asking him questions about his native country, his favorite foods—basically anything that didn't have to do with children or careers. He must have gotten the message because we didn't return to the previous topic.

I distinctly remember this being one of the first nice conversations I had with a stranger that included a discussion of my children after Davey's passing. It took considerable effort, compared to the carefree way I used to talk to strangers, but I felt I was making progress. Though it didn't take long for me to learn how to talk about my son in casual conversations, how I discussed him with people I now met through my consulting practice was a continual work in progress.

After the accident, I decided to focus all of my efforts on my software and management consulting practice. There was plentiful work and it was something I could immerse myself in without having to address many of the challenges I faced with our security start-up business. But this, of course, meant getting out and talking to people. If a discussion became competitive and ego-driven, which many business conversations typically do, I didn't hesitate to pull out the grief hammer and use it to my advantage, often with short-term positive and long-term negative results.

For example, when a potential business partner and I discussed how my technology practice could help his new business concept, we were in the "getting to know each other" mode. He had a successful business and his ego was on full display, constantly countering my experiences with grander versions of his own, which started to rub me the wrong way. When he said he was about to be an empty nester I mentioned that I was already there and, yes, it's hard. That triggered another one-upmanship effort, as he quickly countered with "Well, I'm a single dad raising my daughter so it's really hard...."

I became Captain Grief and pulled out my hammer.

"Wow, yeah, that must be tough. I lost my son in a car accident a few months ago. It's hard being a parent...."

The conversation ended soon after that with the obligatory "I'm so sorry" from him. I quickly realized that he *was* genuinely sorry; the news visibly affected him. I had let my own ego get the better of me and used my grief as a tool to dominate in an alpha male contest that I never should have participated in in the first place.

Needless to say, the potential partnership never went any further.

I had built a career leveraging my skills and experience to help me land new business and open doors. Software engineers are typically very opinionated and love to promote their perspective on why something is "right" or their opinion has more value. If I was going to grow from this experience, I needed to learn to come from a place of peace and love, not anger and pride.

The grief I was processing wasn't some career experience that I could put on a résumé. While it did redefine the majority of my life, I didn't want it to define me. Though I was starting to navigate my way out of the grief and get back out into the world, I clearly had more learning to do.

Friends

I generally have two classes of friends: couples that Allison and I are both very close to and my own friends. The latter are mostly guys that I like to hang out with, the closest being my poker group. We have been getting together once a month for decades and that gathering is a much-needed opportunity to shed my responsibilities and act like a kid. We lob friendly insults at one another, drink a few beers, and try to make everyone laugh to the point where tears come out and stomachs hurt. If you can make a middle-aged man cry from laughter it's a good night.

My friend Bob usually hosts the poker nights and we use his basement as our personal bar and casino. We enter the house through the back door, directly into the basement, avoiding the front door and walking through the grass to get there. I always feel like a teenager, bag of beer in hand, sneaking into a party where the parents are out of town.

The Magnificent Seven (yes, our group has a nickname) have been through a lot together: job changes, copious hair loss, divorces, and the passing of children. Mine was not the first loss of a child. Rich, an occasional member of our group who has long since moved out of state, had lost his teenage son a decade earlier. Rich's tragedy shook me to my core and dramatically impacted the way I looked at my own children. Though Rich moved away he was often on our minds, and he was a common topic of conversation; his presence was missed.

It was only a couple of months after Davey's accident that I resumed playing poker with my friends. That first night back was a little awkward. I wasn't sure that I could play the wise-cracking, sharp-witted, and hilarious card shark that I normally did. Of course, that was my view of myself. My friends would likely say that I'm the Forrest Gump of the group, capable of only simple observations and constantly betting into losing hands.

The reality was, the first night back was a bit somber. I could feel the sadness coming from my friends and the genuine concern they had for me. Noble attempts were made to lighten the mood and laugh. I felt that each of us was trying to figure out how this was going to work.

It's easy to be a friend when everything is going well, but your true friends are the ones that are there for you when everything starts to spin. You reach out to stabilize yourself and they put out a hand to support you, even when you're spinning so hard you take them down too. It was clear that these men were not just feeling sorry for me or viewing me as the damaged goods I felt like. I chose to view them as genuinely caring for me and I wanted to make sure they knew it.

Toward the end of that first evening back, I took advantage of a pause in the game to thank each of them for being there for me. We typically focus on fun and laughter for poker night, but this was not a typical night. I wanted to make sure they knew how much their support meant to me, and how much better they had made me feel. Sometimes it was hard to set the grief aside for even a moment, but doing that and focusing on gratitude seemed to mop up some of the pain I was experiencing.

Men are notoriously bad at demonstrating their feelings, especially to other members of the beer-drinking, football-watching, card-playing, outspoken middle-aged group I belong to. We tend to internalize our problems, package them up and push them way down to be processed later, usually with a generous application of alcohol or sleepless nights replaying the problem over and over again. From that night on, however, my relationship with the Magnificent Seven changed.

I now looked on them not as friends but as brothers. At the end of the evening we would have our usual manly pound shake. This involves grasping the right hand of your friend, bending the elbow down and the hand up, and pulling them toward you. The left hand is then used to simultaneously hug and pummel the back of your friend. Somehow the only way grown men can hug is if some form of violence is involved. Now, however, I often quietly say "I love you, brother." It took a few times but now I sometimes get "Love you too, man" back.

While all of this may sound very touching, I feel safe expressing it to you knowing that the Magnificent Seven rarely read anything that isn't dominated by a periodic swimsuit issue — so it's highly unlikely they will ever encounter these words. If you run across any of my friends, please do me a favor and keep this to yourself.

I do have many other friends, some that I speak with regularly and others that are infrequent connections. I have had a few friends disclose that they had not reached out to me after Davey's passing because they weren't sure how they should act. I told them not to worry, that it's better to say things that may be a little awkward rather than nothing at all; at least it shows that you care and are willing to do something that may be uncomfortable to help a friend. It may take a few conversations to smooth out the relationship but it's worth the effort.

The other group of friends — the couples that Allison and I get together with regularly — are our East Coast family. These are the families that lived near us when we moved to Virginia back in the mid-'90s and have effectively grown up with us over the last twenty-four years. We've each seen our collective children become adults and watched some of them go off, get married, and have their own kids. We've shared many vacations together, and as some couples moved away from the neighborhood we still remain close friends.

This group was the first to show up to our home—en masse. The morning after the accident, the couples showed up together, taking the day off work. When they walked in the door it was like a light came in with them and Allison and I felt immediate relief, which we desperately needed during those, our darkest hours. The rest of our extended family were still in the process of flying and driving to us from all over the country and we had felt so alone and isolated before they appeared.

All they really needed to do to make us feel better was show up, but of course they did so much more. Barbara Fleagle, who the night before had driven our Julia home from the beach, immediately took charge. Finding a place to have a celebration of Davey's life was the last thing Allison and I would have been able to deal with; Barbara grabbed that responsibility and ran with it, calling countless venues and arranging everything.

Each of our friends was devastated by what had happened, not just because they could see our pain but because they had helped raise Davey. This was their loss too. I was not just the manifestation of their worst nightmare, I was a dear friend that they loved, and they would do anything to provide me with comfort.

In the first few months, trying to get together with these couples was difficult. It was hard not to see how much they still had and be reminded of what we had lost. I had been viewing my friends and their families as benchmarks for my own family. It was like seeing someone move into a new home or get a new car and thinking "Wow, I'd like something like that...."

It took considerable effort to change my perspective and see my friends' families through their eyes. Once I did that I was able to experience an even more pronounced joy around my friends than I ever had before. The birth of a grandchild, the engagement of one of the kids, the new businesses they launched — each of these moments they shared became something I felt connected to, not just something I would not experience through Davey.

I didn't feel I was simply living vicariously through my friends — I had become so close to them, I could truly feel their joy and happiness in a much deeper way.

Digital Landmines

Another challenge we faced was how to handle the often intrusive nature of an extensive digital life. Social media is both a blessing and a curse to the newly bereaved; it can be a primary conduit for connecting with friends and family. In our case it allowed us to see all the wonderful acts of kindness people were doing in our son's name, and receive links for inspirational videos and articles.

There were several dark sides to this connectivity, however, among them local news sites and community forums. When the police put out the press release about my son's accident they added at the end that "alcohol may have been a factor," though I knew that Davey had not had anything to drink for at least two days before the accident and there was nothing found at the accident scene to imply that he had. Later the toxicology report would confirm that he had nothing in his system, but it wasn't a news story by then.

Having been online since well before there was an actual Internet, I'm familiar with how brutal people posting anonymously can be. Personally, I avoided using Google to find out what news was out there on my son, and stuck to very limited social media channels. Unfortunately, though, that didn't always help.

When a friend suggested I visit his Facebook page to view his artwork, a picture popped up of Davey and his friend Spencer, from eight years earlier. I had brought them to a Caps hockey game to celebrate Spencer's seventeenth birthday. Facebook suggested posting this happy memory to my timeline.

It was seven months to the day after Davey had passed.

Seeing the smiling face of my son at sixteen was difficult at that point in my journey. I immediately made the calculation that I would, at that point, have eight years and five months left with him physically. If I knew that then, would I have done things differently? These were the thoughts that dominated my mind at that point.

LinkedIn recommended that I log in and congratulate Davey on his one-year work anniversary, a year after he started work with me on our start-up. The email included a picture of Davey in his suit, flashing that big smile of his. I had taken the photo of him a little over a year earlier and I knew that while he looked all dressed up he was actually wearing shorts, since it was just a headshot. While I loved that picture, having some system decide I needed to see it right now wasn't helpful.

Even my iPhone got in on the act, at one point giving me a notification that it had created a new "memory" for me. I could see a little photo of Davey in the message and slid the notification to open it. Suddenly I was witness to a video montage of Davey pictures set to snappy music, wrapping up with the last short video I had made of him—the one I had shown to the police officers to confirm his identity after the accident.

These digital landmines seemed to be everywhere, and I had to learn how to step on them without triggering an explosion of grief.

Figuring out all the various settings to make these notifications stop didn't seem like a solution. There would always be reminders, and trying to make my happiness depend on never seeing them created too many conditions for that happiness.

Recovering from the emotionally difficult parts of grief required that I control what I placed my attention on. It wasn't just some emails and pop-up notifications. I would never see Davey get married or become a father himself, would not get to see him develop his career, go on our backpacking trips or big family vacations. The list of things I was missing out on was huge and everything seemed to bring them up; the reminders were unavoidable.

Initially I tried to address this by focusing on what I did have—an amazing wife, two incredible daughters, a large, loving family, and friends that were always right there for me. While that helped, it didn't last. It just felt like there was this large black hole in our family that I simply couldn't avoid.

It didn't matter how many times I bargained with God or played what-if scenarios, there was nothing in this world that would change the fact that Davey was gone physically. But he was still with me in a very real, spiritual way. I learned that I needed to not just accept that but embrace it.

A counselor from the group Compassionate Friends visited us a few days after the accident and told us that grief was like carrying around a brick in your pocket. It was heavy and painful but after a while you would pat the brick to reassure yourself that it was still there. Frankly, that felt like a sad way to continue through life.

What I needed to do was focus on Davey as he was now; his physical presence was gone but the energy that powered his body was still around. My readings of the afterlife opened the door and my conversation with Davey just a couple weeks after his physical death pushed me through it. When I approached my grief with an open mind and allowed myself to experience what I had previously thought was impossible, I flipped a switch in myself.

I began to accept that Davey's physical life was perfect exactly as it was, from beginning to end. He really had accomplished everything he was meant to accomplish and he did in fact set Allison, the girls, and me on very different paths than we would have been on without him. Everyone encounters challenges and suffering in their life. It's not what happens to us but how we react to it that defines us.

Many times, when feeling a little down, I would remember the day of the accident, that morning on the screened-in porch when Davey came over and hugged me telling me multiple times, "I will never leave you." To say those words haunt me would be a disservice to what I now see as his intent: he didn't leave me. He's still right here.

Signs

Many spiritually oriented people—especially mediums—will tell you that those who have died will visit the ones they left behind. Sometimes it's something subtle, like a wind chime going off when there is no breeze; other times it's noises in a home that are difficult to explain. I struggled initially to believe some of these phenomena when they happened to me.

I often spent time in our backyard, one of Davey's favorite places. Our property has a large yard, with a pool, several ponds, and an abundance of butterfly bushes. During the late summer and into fall we have hundreds of swallowtail butterflies visiting us, as well as dozens of monarchs, painted ladies, colorful moths, etc. It truly is a magical place.

One morning while pacing around the backyard I looked up to see a large monarch butterfly descend from the oak tree in front of me. It glided gracefully, not the usual chaotic flapping, and landed on a bush directly in front of me. Normally monarchs are pretty skittish creatures and it's hard to get too close to them. This one, however, not only allowed me to approach but let me place my finger gently next to it. The Monarch then crawled up on my finger and decided to sit a spell, giving me time to pull out my phone and snap this picture:

After a few minutes of hanging out together I put my finger up to a bush and he crawled off my hand. A sheer state of bliss came over me. It was almost like an electrical reaction—my body felt like it was vibrating—and I clearly sensed Davey was with me right then.

Another time, when coming home one day just a couple weeks after Davey's accident, as I pulled into our driveway and passed the basketball hoop I immediately thought of Davey. More often than not I had to wait, when I pulled up, for Davey to finish his shot, before I could pull into the garage. I paused for a moment and thought of my son and how very much I missed him.

I pulled into the garage then and turned off the engine of my car. That's when I heard it: the very distinct sound of a basketball being dribbled behind me. Looking in the rearview mirror revealed an empty basketball court, yet the sound was clear and distinct.

The moment was a bit surreal—was I hearing things? Did someone run up behind me and start playing basketball? Our closest neighbor was over 500 feet away—was this somehow an echo from one of their kids playing with a ball? The neighborhood had appeared empty when I drove up. No, the sound was clearly coming from the driveway right behind me. I looked to my left and saw Davey's basketball sitting in the bin where it normally resided when he wasn't playing with it—yet I could very clearly hear the sound of a basketball being dribbled on the blacktop behind my car.

I opened the door of my car, half expecting to see Davey out on the driveway shooting hoops. As soon as the door unlatched and opened, the sound stopped. I quickly closed the door again, but the sound was gone. I still had this overwhelming feeling that Davey was right there.

I wasn't the only one experiencing things like this. Julia had multiple dreams where Davey would visit her, both as a kid and as an adult. In one of her early dreams she felt like she was being charged with electricity and woke up physically shaking to hear a voice repeat over and over "Sorry, sorry!"

Davey was the subject of several of Allison's dreams and they were super realistic. In one she was on a bus with the entire extended family and Davey was there. She got excited and yelled out to everyone else on the bus, so happy that Davey was alive and well—but Allison was the only one that could see him. The dreams in which she saw Davey were different than her other dreams—they seemed very realistic and her memory of them didn't fade after waking up like other dreams did.

It wasn't just our family. Davey's best friend, Spencer, had a number of vivid dreams in which Davey visited him, as did other friends from high school and college. The news of these dreams trickled in from different sources as people checked in on us — it seemed clear that Davey was attempting to reach out to a lot of people.

A few months after Davey's accident we received some interesting news. Spencer's older sister had a friend named Lindsey that had just visited a psychic medium in our area named Celeste Woods — and she had received a message from Davey. It seemed odd that someone that barely knew Davey would be connecting to him through a medium but the story she conveyed to us was simply amazing.

Below is the email our daughter Jocelyn received from Lindsey:

```
From: Lindsey Miller
Date: October 17, 2016 at 11:15:57 PM EDT
To: Jocelyn Alison
Subject: Message

Hi Jocelyn,

Below is my recount of the message I received
from Davey. I feel so honored and lucky that I
was able to receive his message and then have the
means to pass it along to you. Of course feel
free to ask me any questions if you need anything
clarified. Sending my love to you and your
family. Hope to see you at Thanksgiving!!

After my arrival, Celeste (the medium) told me a
bit about her process and how the reading would
work. She asked if I was looking to connect with
someone who had passed, seeking life guidance, or
anything else. I told her I was there to just see
```

what came to her...I wasn't in need of a message
from anyone in particular.

Celeste started getting a message from one of my
guides and as she began writing it down she said
"Okay, hold on. I'm trying to receive this
message for you but someone has just stepped
forward and they are relentless and won't stop
until I deliver this to you." She told me it was
a male, about my age, who had recently passed.
She asked if this made sense and I immediately
knew it was Davey. I only said yes and she kept
going by saying "You knew him through school?
He's putting on an athletic type of jacket, which
means to me there's a school connection." Again,
I only said yes. She kept going and said "He
passed tragically and unexpectedly, right? No
long, drawn-out illness or anything. It was an
accident." At that point I just burst into tears,
which...if you ask anybody...does not happen very
often to me. I am never the person to break down
crying but I was just so touched and taken by
surprise (I don't know that Davey and I had ever
even spoken before!) that Davey showed up.

She kept going and said "He's been pestering a
lot of people, trying to get messages across,
right?" I told her he's been visiting a lot of
people in dreams and he passed about two months
ago. She laughed and looked in his direction and
was like "Geez, you're good at this!" Normally
spirits aren't able to connect until about six
months after they've passed, so you should know
he's working hard to connect with people! Celeste
said that he wants me to pass along to his family
that he is doing just fine, he's happy, in no
pain, and he's sorry he had to leave so soon. He
knows the destruction he left behind and he takes
full responsibility. He also said "My poor mom is
a mess. But they're all going to be okay."

She asked me to confirm that he left behind two
sisters. Then she asked if there was anyone who
had a name with "sh" in it, like Shelly or
something along those lines. I told her I wasn't
aware of anyone and that led her to an "S" name,
which I interpreted as Spencer. She said he's
feeling a lot of guilt and feels that if he had

been there he could have saved Davey, but she said that isn't true. It was just his time. She also said Davey was making her look down, which means he was distracted when he was driving and wasn't looking at the road. She mentioned something about a country road, going full speed, but there was no suffering when he passed. It was immediate and he didn't feel any pain. He also said he wasn't alone when he passed, which Celeste took to mean that his spirit guides and angels were with him and helped him pass.

He was very adamant about wanting you and your family to know that he's with you and he's absolutely fine and loves you all. He's going to pass on and isn't stuck in this world, but he's just taking his sweet time getting out of here because he doesn't want to leave you guys yet. He wants to make sure you are all okay before he goes. He also sent me to Celeste because he wants you all to visit her, but Celeste told him it's too soon. She said after six months to a year he can send you to her. He agreed ;-)

The way it ended was by Celeste asking if he had anything else he needed to say and he said nope, that was it! He gave a little wave and then hung out with us for the rest of my time with her.

Also I want you to know that as I was typing all of that out, Davey was with me. My entire body suddenly got warm and tingly and my head started spinning a bit. It's a hard feeling to explain but it was like my brain was trying to receive something that it just didn't know how to translate. So I closed my eyes and asked him what else he wanted me to tell you and the word "love" just popped into my head and I felt extra warm. So passing that along to you, courtesy of Davey!

I really hope this message brings you some form of comfort. Your brother loves you so, so much and I think the fact that he sent me, essentially a stranger, proves that he will stop at nothing to make sure you remember that.
--
Lindsey Miller

Some of these details about Davey's accident had never been discussed outside of our immediate family. The likelihood of the medium doing research on her upcoming client and connecting Lindsey to Davey through an Internet search was extraordinarily remote. It was becoming easier and easier to believe that, fundamentally, Davey was not really gone — that his consciousness had survived his physical death and that us feeling his presence was actually my son trying to connect with us.

Finding Mediums

I'll be honest: as an older, socially conservative guy that had been immersed in software engineering for over three and a half decades, the idea of seeking out a physic medium felt…weird. Prior to Davey's accident I never really thought about mediums. On the rare occasion that the prospect of one came up (Whoopi Goldberg's role in the movie *Ghost* is an example), I assumed it was some kind of con game.

Davey's passing at such a young age left me looking for answers. The conversations I had with him prior to his accident and the things I had personally been experiencing meant getting out of my comfort zone. The Van Praagh book and others I had read were having an impact on me. The idea of seeking out a medium started to feel more and more reasonable.

I did a little research and found the website of Bob Olson (who also has a book called *Answers about the Afterlife: A Private Investigator's 15-Year Research Unlocks the Mysteries of Life After Death*). He has done a lot of research on mediums and has personally tested those that appear on his list. This seemed as good a place as any, for Allison and me to start.

Each medium works a little differently and the one we reached out to offered to do the reading over the phone. Apparently being able to tune in to someone's deceased relative didn't require the sitter (the person receiving the reading) to be physically present.

Another aspect of reaching out to a medium so quickly after a loss is that they will warn you that they can't always connect with the person you want to receive—it's not like placing a call to a specific person. When we did our phone reading with the medium he felt a connection to my mother, who had passed five years earlier. While I was happy to hear from my mom, both Allison and I desperately wanted to hear from our son.

The initial things the medium presented were pretty general, especially as it related to my mom. I would learn later that it is really important to find a medium that is an evidential medium — they present you with information that only the deceased person would be able to share, that would be very difficult to guess. This helps confirm that they are indeed connecting to your family member.

Our first medium wasn't really hitting on evidential details, but instead more general things about how my mom was still a part of my life and that she was working to arrange money to come our way, which sounded very vague. He then began to connect with "the spirit of a young man" and asked if we had lost a son recently; we confirmed that we had.

He then told us a few things about Davey that I would qualify as evidential. The first was that he said at the time of his passing Davey was in an altered state of mind — not drugs or alcohol but that he was experiencing an awakening of some kind. This sounded very much like what Davey was going through in the three days leading up to his accident. He also asked if we had a basketball hoop in the backyard, which we quickly confirmed. He said Davey still plays basketball in the backyard and was showing him an image of making a perfect shot — nothing but net. After hearing that basketball dribbling in the backyard just a few days earlier I felt the medium was really connecting well.

The remainder of the reading went in an odd direction, and both Allison and I felt a little disappointed with the way the medium continued with the session. The reason I don't mention this medium's name is that he is very well respected and I think the quality of the reading had more to do with our impatience in not hearing more from our son. We were so desperate to get clear proof of a connection from Davey that nothing short of "he's telling me his name is Davey, that his birthday is March 20 and that he died on July 20 and that he had two sisters and 10 first cousins" would have made us feel that solid evidence was being presented to us.

I would soon learn that each medium connects in a very different way. Some get very clear visuals, others hear words or see phrases that they are able to convey. Some see symbols that they have learned to associate with specific attributes, events, or personality traits.

An important part of getting a good reading from a medium is the mindset with which you approach the experience. Many mediums will tell you that learning to meditate, to quiet your mind and focus on positive, loving thoughts will help make the connection a medium makes stronger.

Beginning Meditation

Of all the things that helped me navigate through my grief, developing a regular meditation practice was easily the single most important tool I picked up. Frankly, I never thought I would be able to meditate—the inner monologue that drives my thoughts always seemed to have something to ponder, whether it was what needed to be worked on, my likes or dislikes, what I said or needed to say to someone else, etc.—there was always a new thought right behind the last one. It was just too noisy in my head.

In the immediate aftermath of Davey's accident I found that all of my thoughts had suddenly been muted. Everything seemed so trivial compared to the loss of my son; Davey was all I could think of and this brought me extreme pain, initially. The only respite I found was going outside and looking at nature. I could suddenly stare for hours at a tree swaying in the wind without any real thoughts entering my head other than how much I missed and loved my son.

I read Eckhart Tolle's book *The Power of Now* and became consumed with the idea of learning who "I" was. Tolle recounts how he learned that he wasn't his thoughts but the observer of them. That resonated with me as well—I had thoughts that sounded like a third person: "David, you idiot, why did you say that?" I began to learn that my thoughts could be brutally hard on me, often pointing out my flaws, poorly made decisions, or things I said and later regretted.

My brain seemed to enjoy binge-watching negative memories of things I had done, replaying poor decisions over and over again or agonizing over an issue. If I made a mistake, I could be assured of getting every variation on how I had screwed up replayed. When I left my expensive Bluetooth headphones on an aircraft I obsessed about where I had left them, where they probably were now, how much I would need to pay to replace them, why I hadn't just put them in my bag, etc.

I started to see that there was a similarity between the feelings of grief I was experiencing and how I processed negative events in my life. Though the feelings of grief were amplified, they followed a similar pattern, endlessly replaying the negative aspects of losing my son: how much I missed Davey, why this had to happen, what I should have done differently, how I had failed to protect him, etc.

When I had read about meditation in the past it was often associated with quieting the mind. That seemed like an impossible task to me. Sitting quietly with my eyes closed and soft music playing just seemed to trigger even more thoughts. As a software engineer I felt that I had entered an endless loop: how could I think about not thinking?

In the early stages of grief my thoughts were so overcome by the loss of my son that I thought of little else. It was almost as if my brain was being trained to allow some thoughts to enter my head but not engage them—the minutiae of life seemed pointless and while I "heard" those thoughts, they had no emotional impact on me. I simply did not feel them and as a result they stopped replaying in my head.

The constant stream of thoughts had been broken.

Initially I used meditation as a vehicle to communicate with Davey. I would play very gentle music, close my eyes, and focus on breathing. I found that if I focused on how much I missed Davey it didn't help—feelings of sadness and grief would come up. Instead, I placed my attention on how incredibly lucky I was to be Davey's dad and how much I loved him right at that moment, even though he had physically left me.

The results were wonderful. Most of the time I would see myself standing on a beach. Perfectly formed waves would be breaking and then I'd see Davey next to me, staring out at those perfect waves. I would greet him and tell him how much I missed him and he would often come back with "Why do you miss me? I'm right here!"

We didn't have too many conversations—just being in his presence was so incredibly comforting. Every once in a while he would say "Come on, Dad, let's go!" The next thing I knew we'd be flying side by side over incredible landscapes or surfing in the waves. Davey would be his usual athletic self and perform tricks on his surfboard. He loved showing me how he could now fly.

Meditation was opening a door to Davey's world and allowing me to connect to him. It was also helping me in other ways—suddenly my stress levels were dropping. When I had gone to my doctor about a month after Davey's accident he had not very helpfully offered to provide me with some prescriptions to assist with sleep and the ability to focus. The idea that I needed to be sedated or medicated was not something I wanted to entertain.

After a couple months of regular meditation, my blood pressure—always a little high because of the stress of my work—had dropped into a healthy range. I felt so much calmer and better able to handle the daily challenges of a busy life. Navigating through the grief had left me with a different perspective on what was really important, but the bulk of the calming influence on my life I attributed to meditation.

The meditation and regular sessions in which I connected with Davey were a huge help to me emotionally. I would soon learn to lean on these new skills very heavily—apparently the challenges in my life wouldn't end with Davey's passing.

250 Days

In late October 2016, just a few months after Davey's accident, Allison and I went out with some friends for dinner. After the meal we stopped by a local brew pub and tried to act like normal people, though it was still tremendously difficult. We are long-term members of the community and Allison has been a local high school teacher for over fifteen years, so that meant we always ran into someone we knew, often for the first time since Davey's accident. That night was no exception.

Several young men stopped by and said hello and wanted to express their sympathies. Among them was Connor Calderwood, one of Davey's classmates in high school. Connor had grown up down the street from us and he and Davey often played together as young children. He told us how sorry he was that he couldn't make it to Davey's service because he was in Alaska working as a fisherman.

An outgoing, upbeat, and joyful young man, Connor did his best to cheer us up, telling funny stories about his adventures in Alaska as well as some memories of he and Davey growing up. We chatted with him for a while, then he embraced each of us with a big bear hug and left with his friends. Connor was different than many of the people that expressed their sympathy — he had an infectious way of expressing happiness and it was just a pleasure to be with him.

Just a couple months later, on January 3, we would learn that Connor had passed away. He was twenty-five years old.

Allison and I decided that we needed to show support for Connor's family and we attended his funeral service. It was extremely difficult because not only was everyone in a very somber mood, when they encountered us they really struggled to contain their emotions, which was a challenge for both Allison and me.

I was so proud of the way Allison held it together, knowing it was very difficult for her to manage the complex emotions of grief while surrounded by so many grieving people. Many of the young people that came up to us were students of hers or the parents of those students, looking to her both for comfort and to express their sympathy. Personally, I was really struggling to maintain any semblance of composure.

One of the families we saw at Connor's funeral was the Pollocks. We had known Sofia and Eric for over fifteen years; their oldest son, Harrison, was Davey's age (twenty-four) and I had coached him for many years in youth sports. He and Davey had been on many teams together and Harrison always had a warm smile on his face, regardless of what was happening. Harrison came up and gave me a hug, just as he had done a few months earlier at Davey's memorial.

We chatted for a bit but the emotions were difficult for me to control so I kept our conversation pretty short. Two weeks later we would learn that Harrison had died suddenly of an unknown heart condition.

In the course of six months, three young men from the same high school class had passed.

I found myself in new territory, trying to make sense of what had happened and trying desperately to help the young friends of Davey's, faced with the loss of so many of their peers in such a short period of time. It felt as though the visits we received from Davey's friends were not just courageous attempts to give us comfort, but an opportunity for them to find answers as well.

I could not attend Harrison's funeral—I had booked a trip to California to visit my dad, whose health had been failing rather rapidly. My dad's health had been a problem for a couple of years; he was an alcoholic for most of his life as well as a heavy smoker—combine that with being an insulin-dependent diabetic and frankly I was surprised he had made it to eighty years old.

After my mom passed away I had begun to have a much better relationship with my dad; I spoke to him often on the phone and tried to visit him as often as I could. When I showed up to see him this time, it became pretty clear that my dad's days on earth were numbered. He was in the hospital and had experienced what we believed was a stroke, leaving him bedridden and barely lucid.

Each day when I stopped by to see him he was sleeping. He would wake occasionally but just gaze around the room and not seem to see my brother or me. On the last day of my visit I was standing by his bedside and reached out and placed my hand gently on his head. He opened his eyes and looked directly into mine, smiled, and mouthed the words "I love you."

It was the last time I would see my dad alive.

Back home in Virginia on March 27, at 3:52 a.m. I received a text message from my brother:

"Hey man, Dad passed at 12:35 a.m."

In the course of 250 days I had lost my son and my father—both carried the same name as me. I had also experienced the loss of two of Davey's friends, young men that should have had more time on this planet, just as Davey should have. Or so I thought at the time.

I'm convinced that going through what I had with Davey, and then with Connor and Harrison, prepared me to handle my dad's passing. It still hurt, of course, and I shed some tears, but I was able to focus on my dad in a completely different way. I would soon learn that some of the feelings my dad had for me would become more apparent.

Reflections on My Father

I had an awkward relationship with my dad when I was growing up. My mom was the epitome of selfless love for her children, while my dad had…issues. His own father, the first of the Davids in our family, was a handsome man, an actor that could charm anyone. His mother was a sharp and successful marketing executive for CBS. The black and white photos of them with my dad and his younger sister presented an iconic lifestyle with celebrity friends and all the glamour that Hollywood had to offer in the 1930s.

What those photos didn't tell was the real story of how my grandparents' relationship was strained at best and led to divorce in the 1940s. My grandfather quickly remarried, his new wife an heiress to the Coca Cola family fortune. With this newfound wealth my grandfather purchased a large ranch near Santa Barbara, California, which they renamed Rancho Cola.

My dad lived with his mother until the age of fourteen, and then decided to leave Hollywood and become a cowboy on his father's ranch while attending high school. He would do that for the next four years, leading tours on this working dude ranch and enjoying all that Rancho Cola had to offer. One fateful day his horse stepped into a gopher hole at full gallop, rolled, and he became caught up in the saddle. The impact would tear the muscles and ligaments in his leg apart and give him a significant head injury. He was in a coma for weeks after that accident and required muscle and skin grafts to help him fully recover.

While all this was happening, my grandfather and his wife were recovering from a long series of poor financial decisions and the failure to pay their taxes; as a result they lost their ranch and both moved on from my father's life. One day my dad was riding his horse on the family ranch, his future secure and well defined. He woke up with a broken body and everything he thought he had was suddenly gone.

He was soon drafted into the army and served as a rifleman in the infantry, spending most of his time stationed in Germany during the late 1950s and early '60s. There he developed a taste for alcohol and though he honorably served his country, he left the service with a drinking problem. He soon met and fell in love with my mom, and she became the stabilizing force my dad desperately needed, bringing with her a strong sense of family that my dad never had growing up.

Since both my mom and dad worked blue collar jobs to keep the family going, my grandmother on my mom's side — Nana — came to live with us and helped raise my brother and me. My dad loved Nana as if she was his own mother, though he had his own peculiar way of showing it.

Usually charming and funny, when my dad really "hit the sauce" his behavior would become boorish and awkward. He would drink a little in the morning before work, then have a few drinks immediately after work, drive home (usually drunk), and then drink himself into a stupor in front of the TV every single night. He was never violent or even argumentative, just completely intoxicated every night. In retrospect I'm amazed his body even survived what he put it through.

More than a couple times, my dad got into a car accident after work. This was the 1970s and back then in Los Angeles drivers were never cited for drunk driving. The police would simply show up at our door and drop my dad off. They would hand my mom the police report for the accident he had caused—usually hitting a parked car—and let her deal with the aftermath.

I clearly remember being an eleven-year-old boy and playing football out in the front yard. An errant bounce of the football hit my hand in an odd way and it badly displaced my pinky finger, pushing the bone back into the palm of my hand. My Italian grandmother didn't drive or speak English and this was in the days before mobile phones, so she wrapped my hand in ice and waited for my parents to get home.

As I lay there in incredible pain my dad got home first, in his usual state of inebriation. My grandmother pulled him into my room and he reached down, clumsily inspected my badly disfigured finger, and simply said "Yep, that's broken." He then turned around and walked out, going next door to continue knocking back rounds of whiskey with our neighbor, one of his regular drinking buddies. An hour later my mom got home from work, took a quick look at my mangled hand, and rushed me to the emergency room. My finger was never the same after that and even today has an odd shape from being out of the socket for so long.

It took me many years to forgive my dad for that incident and it was a formative memory of our relationship. The message I learned early was that the drinking was more important than I was.

However, my dad had other qualities I greatly admired. He was always giving us homespun advice about hard work, doing a job right the first time, and being grateful for what we had, especially food. Much later in life I would often find myself repeating his advice to my own children, as much as I had difficulty admitting it came from my dad.

My father was also the least racist person I had ever met, though I also didn't appreciate that until later. Growing up in

Los Angeles in the late sixties and early seventies meant being aware of racial division, but that never came from my family; my dad's friends were of every race and ethnic background. He simply liked everyone, especially if they would sit down and have a few drinks with him.

As I grew into a young man I distanced myself from my dad. As a teenager any time I brought around friends or—even worse—a girlfriend, he would embarrass me in some excruciating way. When I met my wife I made sure to limit her exposure to him as much as possible, not wanting her to think that this was what I would become.

When Allison became pregnant with our first child I gave my dad an ultimatum: I told him that if he continued to drink, I would not be bringing his granddaughter anywhere near him. I did not want my daughter exposed to that.

To my dad's credit, he quit drinking cold turkey after I told him that. While my mom, brother, and I had worked on him for years about getting sober, it was the thought that he would never see his grandchildren that led him to stopping this behavior completely. He never had another alcoholic drink again. It was by far my proudest moment as my father's son and became not just a turning point in our relationship but also in the quality of his life.

I share my father's story with you because I found it wasn't just my son I was connecting with from the afterlife.

An Engineer's Dilemma

Intellectually, I really struggled when I started to make the shift to believing in the afterlife. Though I had experiences that I knew deep down were very real, as an engineer I have a healthy respect for a science-based approach. I wanted to know that what I was experiencing was at least possible, if not directly proven.

Many mainstream scientists — and most atheists — believe that consciousness is simply a byproduct of the human body. According to this theory, all thoughts, feelings, and emotions are caused by chemical reactions in the brain, and when the human body dies those functions cease. For all intents and purposes the human body is no different than a complex machine, and physical death is akin to pulling the cord out of the wall on that machine.

This felt right to me because of the way I experienced life. I had always related to my thoughts as being something that my brain manufactured, and outside of the sensory input from my body, all of my consciousness "felt" like it was happening in my head. If I was going to really believe the afterlife existed I needed to answer those nagging questions.

This was a fundamental difference between my wife and me. Whereas I would try to intellectualize everything that happened and look for the reasons behind events, my wife would feel them in her heart, a concept I had a hard time adapting to. As she had mystical experiences and connections to our son, she seemed to appreciate them more deeply and then move on, looking for the next sign or experience.

It was different for me; everything that happened would trigger my "But why?" reaction. As a child I took apart machines to understand how they worked. As a teenager I worked on my own cars, replacing parts and effectively learning how to be a mechanic. I have always had an insatiable desire to understand things at a level where I could fix or improve them.

For over three decades I had built or been a part of building progressively larger computer systems, to run various businesses. Computer systems require an increasingly large set of dependencies in order to function. The work of hundreds of thousands of engineers is leveraged in even the most simple of computer programs, when you consider all the hardware and software involved. When something fails you have to become brutally efficient at breaking things down until the source of the problem becomes evident.

This process is very similar to what many reductionists and materialists use when trying to explain how life works, and I understood the "why" behind that. The problem is that while the physical world can be observed, weighed, and measured to help validate certain principles of physics, it breaks down when it crosses into the quantum realm.

The more I read on this topic, the more it made sense and helped enable an entire range of phenomena that traditional science had judged fallacious or fraudulent. I started to embrace a mental model of consciousness that viewed the brain as part quantum receiver, capable not only of localized thought but also of being able to access memories and connections at an energetic level.

My perspective changed and my computer analogy was expanded to view my brain as not just a computer capable of generating new thoughts and understanding experiences, but one that was also connected wirelessly to a vast consciousness that I was able to tap into when I quieted my active mind and simply listened.

I continued to look around for evidence that this was provable in some way. The engineer in me was starting to accept it as possible but wanted something a little more solid than theories.

I found two examples that were difficult to ignore, trivialize, or even explain using the traditional "brain only consciousness" models. Both came from long-term studies conducted by the University of Virginia School of Medicine's Division of Perceptual Studies. Founded over fifty years ago by Dr. Ian Stevenson, the division rigorously evaluates empirical evidence that suggests consciousness survives physical death and that the mind and brain are separate.

They have compiled extensive evidence, which I found compelling, in two areas: reincarnation and near-death experiences. In the cases related to reincarnation, there was an undeniable consistency demonstrated. Many children between the age of two (or old enough to communicate) and about seven years old would remember a previous life, often in very specific detail. They could recall family members from the previous life, names of people, names of places, and most often, how they had died.

Another consistently documented aspect was that if the previous life included a violent death, the child would sometimes have a birthmark or birth defect that closely matched how the previous life had ended. In one example, a child had a completely malformed ear and one side of his face was heavily scarred; the person whose life he claimed to remember had been killed by a shotgun blast to that side of his head.

In many cases the UVA team was able to track down the details of the previous person's life and to verify many of the specifics. By the age of about seven the memories of those past lives would fade, and any behavioral issues the child was experiencing related to the previous life tended to disappear as well.

The other area that the UVA team researched was near-death experiences (NDEs). While not everyone that clinically dies has a near-death experience, the ones that do experience key points: being free of pain, leaving the body, clarity of thought, being drawn into a tunnel or darkness, a brilliant light, a life review, etc. I found myself fascinated by this concept and read several books and articles about it, and listened to numerous interviews with people who shared what they had experienced.

While it's possible, however unlikely in my mind, that a brain could manufacture such an experience when a person's body was physically shutting down, one aspect of some NDEs was much more difficult to explain: veridical NDEs. A veridical NDE occurs when a person experiences clinical death, leaves their body, and is able to see and hear verifiable events that are happening while they are "dead." It can be what someone is doing in another room nearby, or it can be a family member thousands of miles away.

One example I found fascinating was the near-death experience of a young woman that had been blind since birth. She had no experience seeing anything in her life yet when she "died" and left her body she could "see" everything around her, the clothing and hospital bands she had on (and their colors), the hospital she was staying in, and other details that were impossible for her to see.

Many people that experience an NDE come out of it very changed. They tend to have a very deep and positive transformation in their life. Most no longer fear death, develop a more loving attitude toward others, have a sense of inner peace and purpose in life — similar to what I was feeling after I got through the grief of my son's passing. All of this just felt very, very familiar.

One thing I found interesting is what would happen when I discussed these topics with friends of mine that have a strong atheist mindset. When I would explain my new view of the afterlife and what I had experienced, many of them would become visibly uncomfortable. Initially I thought it was because I was challenging their beliefs in a way that they found difficult to rationalize, but I soon learned that was usually not the case; they just didn't want to hurt my feelings or puncture a belief system that was clearly bringing me comfort. While I deeply appreciated their concern for my well being, I was surprised to find that even the most intellectually curious people have limits to what they will discuss when a friend's happiness is on the line.

It also made me realize that what I believed — truly believed — wasn't dependent on anyone else believing it.

Seeing Davey Again

It was freezing outside—around 20 degrees Fahrenheit during our pre-dawn hike. John, Spencer, and I had climbed up the Maryland Heights trail with headlamps on and reached the overlook to Harper's Ferry, West Virginia. We took some photos and stood watching the light of the sun slowly paint the town below us. I started to think about Davey, as I often do around John and Spencer.

The Brookbank family has been one of the many groups of people that have been a life raft for the girls and me as we have ridden the waves of grief since Davey's accident. It's hard to describe the joy I find in the company of families like theirs.

The Brookbanks are a mirror image of our family: they had three children (girl, boy, girl) that were the same age as our children. While the older and younger girls were friends with each other, our boys were best friends and pretty much inseparable.

In high school they both played football their freshman year; Spencer was the starting quarterback, Davey the starting running back. When they graduated high school they were chosen "Best Friends" by their class and appeared in the yearbook together.

Davey, Spencer, John, and I had gone on a backpacking trip in the fall before Davey's accident and it was something we all looked forward to doing again, though we never got the chance. After Davey transitioned, John, Spencer, and I carried on the tradition, doing backpacking trips and day hikes. Around the campfire on overnight trips we always have a

110

toast to Davey; a quick sip of bourbon and a moment of quiet reflection on my son.

I looked over at John and Spencer, on the overlook. The love between them was obvious, even in the subtle way males express it. Watching them together made me appreciate the relationship I had with my own son. Just a few months earlier, seeing a father and son together would have made me feel my loss even more; now I was able to appreciate the tremendous gift John and Spencer had, not with envy or jealousy, but with a deep gratitude for being a part of their moment.

I heard a voice in my head: "I'm right here!"

It was unmistakably Davey's voice, and he repeated it several times. I felt him standing right there with us. As the sun rose higher we continued our ascent up the mountain. I was in the lead and as we hit a long rocky climb I suddenly had the urge to move faster. As I picked up my pace, I felt that Davey was there.

That's when I saw him.

Davey was walking on the trail, not twenty yards ahead of me, wearing shorts and turning around and waving for me to keep up. I heard "Come on, Dad!" clearly in my head.

When I looked closely at the trail ahead I couldn't see him, but as soon as I put all my focus on walking quickly up the rocky trail I would catch glimpses of him turning back to look at me and waving me up to him. It was as though I was seeing him in my mind and it was as clear as if I was looking directly at him.

The first thought I had wasn't that I was seeing a ghost or experiencing some kind of hallucination—it was that he was wearing shorts and it was so cold outside. That was the part that didn't make sense to me. Go figure. Always his dad, I guess.

As I scrambled up after Davey I turned and saw that John and Spencer had fallen behind. Only then did I realize that I was nearly running in my frantic effort to catch up to my son. By the time I reached the crest of the trail I was exhausted. I stopped and waited for John and Spencer to catch up, while taking in a stunning overlook of the river winding off into the distance.

I felt Davey was still around us, even though I couldn't see him; his energy was jumping around the three of us as we took in the view. There was no doubt in my mind that Davey had accompanied us on that hike.

A month later I took a nice walk on Easter morning at Seneca Park, a heavily wooded area near our home that runs along the Potomac. It was a delightful day and I had to make it quick since we were meeting our girls and some friends for brunch in Georgetown a few hours later. The weather was simply incredible, everything was flowering and butterflies were frequent companions on my journey.

As I alternated between walking and jogging through the woods I hit a very isolated part of the trail. I had my iPhone playing a very spiritual playlist I often listen to on solo hikes, and the soundtrack from the movie *Avatar* kicked in. The deep percussion of the drums, the sweeping vibrations of the strings, and the choir's voices always give me a boost while running and I felt as though I was flying through the woods.

Sunlight was streaming in through the trees and I was completely caught up in the splendor of my surroundings and focused on how beautiful nature was. Suddenly I felt Davey's presence. He was running right along with me through the trees. I had this wonderful sensation—just utter bliss as he ran alongside me. I couldn't see him like I had during last month's hike, but I knew he was right there.

As I continued to run I felt another presence with me, and this time I could see my dad! He was riding a horse, was very thin, and looked to be in his late teens. He was wearing a white cowboy hat, a long-sleeve white shirt, and jeans. As I ran he galloped through the trees, not worried about the terrain, which for me was a tight and winding trail. One of the last detailed conversations I had with my dad was about his time on the family ranch; even as his mental acuity faded his memories and passion for that time were always very strong.

Suddenly my dad's appearance changed. He was on the same horse, but he was in his mid-fifties, a little bit of a gut but not much. He was dressed as I always remember him—a short-sleeve button-down shirt tucked in, suspenders, and Levi's. He didn't have a hat on now but he was flashing that huge smile of his.

I was just in awe of how amazing this all was. After a short time I couldn't see him anymore and wondered if I had just imagined all of it. As I rounded a tight curve in the trail I came across a huge pile of fresh horse dung, which I barely managed to avoid. In my mind I heard my dad say "See? I really was here!" Dad always had a way of showing the funny side of things.

I slowed to a fast walk, feeling completely at peace. It dawned on me that I would probably never see my mom running alongside me—she wouldn't run under any circumstances. As soon as I thought this I felt my mom's presence, turned my mental attention to my right, and there she was. She wasn't running or riding a horse, she was in her blue 1963 Chevy Impala. She looked just like she did back in the '70s, with her beehive hairdo, driving in the car and smiling over at me. She was radiant and I could see a glow around her.

put my attention on her while trying to continue my jog I
ızed that there was someone in the front seat with her. My
grandmother was there! Nana just leaned forward, looked
right at me, smiled, and waved. She had her purse sitting on
her lap and looked just as I remembered her. The feeling came
over me that my mom was taking my grandmother to an
Easter church service.

At this point in my run I turned left up a very steep
embankment, huffing and puffing with the effort. The images
of my family were no longer there, but the feeling of love from
them remained. I finished my run with the sun streaming
through the trees.

Why have I been able to connect with my son and other family
members across the veil? I believe it's because my meditation
sessions were helping me learn to be more present and turn
off the constant chatter of my brain. I had been making a
strong effort toward mindfulness and absorbing the moment I
was in, especially on my frequent hikes out in the woods.

I was also becoming convinced that life was about far more
than just the physical existence I had previously thought was
all there was. Giving myself permission to believe in an
afterlife opened a window that provided me with tremendous
comfort and a better perspective on the life I had in front of
me.

Growing Together

At the time of Davey's accident Allison and I had been married thirty years. Our relationship had always been strong, which was a huge help to both of us. Anyone that has been married for any length of time knows that being able to stay together isn't just about love—it requires communication, compromise, and genuine respect for your partner.

While Allison and I both had experienced little bumps in our years together, they always seemed to make us closer. We had a synergy that was constantly in balance; when I was down, Allison had the strength to pull me up, and vice versa. We could each tell when the other wasn't happy and would do our best to understand what was at the source of that. We both learned a long time ago that it wasn't either of our job to make the other person happy, but to learn what was really wrong and adjust as needed.

This grief, however, threw us both into a pit at the same time, and neither of us had the strength to comfort the other. Instead we suffered in silence those first few days, comforted only by knowing that the other was right there going through the same thing.

Allison had been on a spiritual journey for nearly a decade, following the teachings of people like Dr. Wayne Dyer and Abraham Hicks. She had been on that journey without me, going to the occasional workshop and filling her shelves with books and audio CDs for those long car rides.

She had never exposed this world to me and frankly I understood why. It appeared on the surface to be some kind of New Age thing that I didn't care to understand and Allison was comfortable keeping it to herself. Just as I had sports to occupy my spare time, Allison had a significant portion of the Hay House library at her disposal.

But while sports can be entertaining and tell an amazing and beautiful story, they're not that helpful in processing grief. Allison overcame her reservations about sharing her world with me and I decided to jump in head first, swimming in the spiritual deep end. I was not at all in my comfort zone but grief had redefined what comfort meant. Plus, having something that Allison and I could learn together became a touchstone for us. We had to communicate constantly, even if just to ensure we weren't both buying the same books.

We also saw this as a lifelong expedition of discovery for the two of us. We shared tips we had learned about being more effective in meditation, told each other about the signs we had seen and most of all how we were both connecting with our son across the veil. Every day became an opportunity to grow a little closer together.

It wasn't just books, websites, and stories we shared; we also started going to workshops together. The gruff old man in me felt like a fish out of water at these events, since the ratio of men to women was often dramatically skewed toward the female demographic. Since my personal demographic (white, middle-aged males) have the highest suicide rate in the US, perhaps I shouldn't assume that water is very healthy for a fish like me anyway.

Since Davey's accident we've been on several weekend retreats to learn from mediums, on a cruise that included spiritual workshops, and have started to attend local support groups together. I've even been seen in small shops that sell incense, crystals, and spiritual books. Was I excited about doing this initially? No. But it meant a lot to Allison and as a result it meant a lot to me—so I ignored the awkwardness of the situation and decided to embrace it.

The results for us were fantastic. Allison was no longer the only one to identify new retreats and spiritual trips; I started offering up venues as well. Our daughters have been very much a part of this process of healing too. From the beginning of this journey the girls have become even closer, both to us and to each other. Allison and I have included them in the planning for some of our spiritual retreats, though this has been decidedly more of a parent activity.

Allison and I have a group text message with our girls titled "The five of us"—we share signs that we find, long-lost pictures or videos of Davey that we discover, anything that allows us to pull together. The five of us continue to be a recurring theme. It's an acknowledgement that Davey is still very much a part of our life.

And something else happened that I did not expect. Tattoos.

While tattoos have become incredibly mainstream, I still found them a little odd. Growing up in Los Angeles in the '60s and '70s, tattoos were either for guys in the Navy or Marines, or something gangbangers sported. Though I had become far less judgmental about them, tattoos still had a stigma that prevented me from ever considering one for myself. Permanently marking up my body? Small needles embedding ink under my skin? No, thank you very much.

In the immediate aftermath of Davey's passing, several of his fraternity brothers got tattoos. Each incorporated surfing (Davey's preferred activity) and Davey's initials. Suddenly three young men that I barely knew were walking around with a permanent memorial for my son on their bodies.

Next Julia went and got a very small tattoo of a wave with Davey's name on it just below her waistline, in a spot that was almost always covered by a bathing suit. Shortly after Julia got hers, Jocelyn got a more elaborate tattoo on the back of her neck, again with the wave theme, though this one was usually covered by her long, thick hair.

I immediately began to want a memorial for my son as well. I grabbed one of my favorite pictures of Davey, holding his board while walking out into the surf, and gave it as a concept to a local tattoo artist named Nina Jean. I also told her I wanted to incorporate a little homage to my father and grandfather as well. Since Davey was David Reese Alison IV, I had the roman numerals I, II, III, and IV placed on the edges surrounding the tattoo. The initials DRA that we all shared were emblazoned on the surfboard itself.

Getting the tattoo wasn't bad at all, far less painful than I was expecting. It was inked on my upper right shoulder, just above the sleeve line, in a shaded single color, and covered most of the ball of my shoulder. I was immediately enamored with it — the artist had done an outstanding job and I couldn't stop looking at it every chance I got.

That seemed to open the floodgates and soon we all decided to get a family tattoo together. The "Five of Us" was a recurring theme and we wanted that to be incorporated. We collectively decided on a hand displaying American sign language for "I love you," with a heart as the palm of the hand. The five fingers represented each of us.

On the first anniversary of Davey's accident we all went to a little tattoo shop in Delaware and got our tattoos. The girls and Allison each got a small version of that tattoo on the inside of their wrist in a pretty visible place, while I got mine on the inside of my left bicep in a much larger size. Allison even surprised me by getting an additional tattoo on her ankle—a monarch butterfly that had "Davey" next to it, in script.

The change I was seeing in my family was profound. We had jumped off the treadmill that was our old life and begun to embrace some change. Not only was it healing, it gave us something significant to look forward to doing together.

Helping Parents Heal

In our search for resources to help us learn more about the afterlife, we came across the group Helping Parents Heal (HPH). They focus on helping parents that have lost a child find comfort through spiritual connections, something very unique among the support groups we had found.

Other grief support groups seem to focus on talking through and sharing the loss. That may work for some people, but Allison and I found that it seemed to just pull us back into our sadness, not lift us up. We had already started down a spiritual path for reconnecting to Davey and in finding HPH we discovered a network of people that we could be completely transparent with. Being able to talk to others openly about the afterlife—even when we all have slightly different takes on it—is a wonderful feeling.

HPH had a Facebook group that helped parents connect, but we really became interested when a new local chapter got started up in our area by Colleen Smith. Colleen had lost her son Austin not long after Davey's accident and they were close in age. We would end up becoming friends with Colleen and her husband, Doug, and we all shared many of our stories about signs, connections, and resources.

Initially attending the group was difficult since the grief was pretty fresh for all of us; over time it got easier, but it could be difficult when new members came and shared their heartbreaking stories and feelings. Eventually we did settle in, however, and were able to detach from others' grief, while still listening to their stories and offering perspectives. I like to think we were becoming role models for how to be happy again after suffering a loss so great.

There were many things that we discovered from that group, not the least of which was how parents dealt with death by suicide. Several members had lost children through suicide, which carries an extra burden on top of an already difficult loss.

I had always used the term "committed suicide" up until I learned the additional negative connotation associated with it. "Commit" in this context is synonymous with "committing" a crime or a murder—so using that phrase had the power to heap yet another judgment on top of a grieving parent's plate. These things are subtle, but when trying to help people navigate what is likely the single most difficult challenge of their life, understanding and navigating these subtleties can be a kindness.

Personally, I had started to feel good about how I was handling the grief. Being able to share resources that gave me comfort was just a natural fit for me. I've always enjoyed helping people and this felt like an outlet for doing exactly that, especially since I now had the ability to come from a place of happiness.

As time went by, friends started to reach out to me on behalf of one of their friends that had lost a child. They had seen how well Allison and I were dealing with things and they hoped we could offer advice and counsel, something I really enjoyed doing. The single most important thing that I would share was that it was going to be okay. This was something that Allison and I both sought early on: we knew the horrible pain would lessen eventually, but would we ever be able to be happy again?

Seeing that there was a light in the darkness was something I truly wanted to share. It also became the main motivation for this book.

Allison's Reading

Both Allison and I had been doing a lot of reading about the afterlife and there was one medium in particular that we both found interesting. Suzanne Giesemann was an author and had written a book called *Messages of Hope* that we really enjoyed, so Allison reached out to her to see if she could schedule a reading, and was added to Suzanne's rather lengthy waiting list.

Suzanne is a compelling person, and her background was a key reason I was interested in Allison getting a reading from her. Suzanne retired after a career as a US Navy Commander, serving as a commanding officer. She had also served as the aide to the Chairman of the Joint Chiefs of Staff and was in that role during the events of 9/11. It was this background that gave Suzanne a high degree of credibility for both Allison and me.

She had retired and was sailing around the world with her husband (also a retired Navy commanding officer) when tragedy hit: Suzanne's stepdaughter was struck by lightning and died instantly, along with the child she was pregnant with. This would lead to a change in the life trajectory of Suzanne and her husband, Ty. Years later she would learn that she had the ability to communicate with people that have passed, and over time she built up that skill to become a very popular medium.

In April of 2017 Suzanne gave Allison a reading over Skype. I was not involved in the video call, but Suzanne provided us with a recording so both of us could listen to it later.

After a few minutes of explanation and a brief pause to get into a deeper state of awareness, Suzanne was able to start providing information to Allison. She knew that she wα attempting to connect with a child but that was all — Allison gave her no indication of gender, age, what happened, etc.

As Suzanne began to bring forth details she said, "Your child is stepping aside and a father figure is coming forward." She tried to refocus on our child, but she said the father figure was very adamant and needed to come forth and apologize — that it felt like a father figure, possibly a father-in-law. She continued to try and refine the connection but she wasn't sure, finally asking Allison if her father was on the other side. When she said no, that it was indeed her father-in-law, Suzanne seemed to hone in much more clearly. She talked about how he had a drinking problem and that he wanted to say he was sorry because he had not supported his son (meaning me) emotionally.

Suzanne continued to bring forth my dad's messages, confirming that he had a military background. She said he wanted to express how proud he was of me, which was something my dad constantly said to me, in virtually every conversation I had with him as an adult.

What she said to Allison next floored me: "He wants to say that your husband turned his back on his father and now he understands why. He's sorry he wasn't more open but he had his own issues to deal with. He's okay now and sees things from a different perspective. He wished he could have had another go at it because he would have been closer. He's showing me how his son had a desire to have more of a father figure and he's sorry he wasn't that. He said he wants him to know that he loves him with all his heart and that he's sorry he wasn't able to show him that."

He then stepped back from Suzanne's focus.

ned to this portion of the recording, I started to
ery emotional. It was one thing to know that my
ho had just passed away the month before—was
mmunicate to me across the veil. It was another
thing for him to realize that he didn't fulfill the role I was
looking for as a child, and that he felt the need to apologize so
adamantly.

I started to realize that I am the person I am today because of
the way my dad was with me—and frankly I liked the person
I had become. He played a critical role in my life, and all I
wanted to do at this point was offer silent thanks to my father
for helping me be a better dad. He really had nothing to
apologize for.

She then started to connect with our child. She said, "I'm
being given the name David. If you know whose name that
is..." Allison interrupted her and immediately said, "That's
my son's name, though he goes by Davey." This led Suzanne
to say, "Well that's just about as awesome as it gets for me...."

Next she covered a couple of things she was getting that were
off-base, or at least they didn't resonate with Allison. She then
said it seemed that his passing was sudden and unexpected
and felt vehicular to her, which Allison confirmed.

Davey then told her that he had not been drinking. Suzanne
said, "He's very emphatic that he had not been drinking,
though he said his mom knows this." She said that she felt he
was driving home from a party, and when Allison said no,
that's not correct, Suzanne said that was okay, they would set
that aside then and move on.

Suzanne picked up a number of other details about the
accident in the reading, from him suffering head trauma, to
him being thrown from his car, to the car having hit a tree.
Once these details came in, Suzanne was on a roll and the

information came more easily. "I'm seeing him swerving as if to avoid something that's coming up at him" — which Allison confirmed.

The number of hits she got was impressive: the kind of work he was doing at the time, the IT nature of his occupation, and how he collaborated with me in business. She was not 100 percent correct in her hits, but some were just really impressive and virtually impossible to guess given the range of options. Davey told her that he had been sending butterflies to the family and was showing her a butterfly landing on someone's hand, which both my daughters and I had experienced in our backyard.

Davey gave her dozens of other pieces of information that was spot-on, and some that demonstrated how Davey had leveraged Suzanne's past experiences as a vehicle for communication. Suzanne relayed that Davey had two sisters and told us that Julia was attending George Mason University and that Jocelyn was living in Georgetown. She tried to provide the name of the college that Davey had attended but it would not come to her, only that it was located in Virginia and he showed himself driving Route 66 to get there. Finally Allison told Suzanne that he had attended James Madison University. Suzanne laughed and said she didn't realize there was a James Madison University in Virginia and that must have been why it was so hard to pull the name out.

Davey also relayed that he knew about the trip to California that Jocelyn and I were about to embark on. Suzanne said that Davey was showing her that I had recently handwritten a contract of some type; just a couple days before I had handwritten a rather lengthy sales contract for a truck I had purchased from someone.

It seemed to me that Suzanne was essentially tuning in to a frequency on a radio, and that when she relayed something

125

that Allison was able to immediately confirm it would result in a stream of details that were also accurate. If she offered up something that Allison indicated was incorrect, Suzanne would then adjust and have a few misses before she got back on the right frequency.

After I reviewed the reading with Suzanne, I wrote an email to her, confirming some of the details of the session that Allison was not sure about but that I could confirm. Suzanne graciously provided a rather lengthy response that included a "drop-in" from Davey. As she was reading my email, Davey came to her and provided some more validation, from meals I had just eaten the day before to what was going on currently with both of our daughters.

Davey clearly remains a very active participant in our lives. For both Allison and me, this reading reinforced that the connection we still felt with our son wasn't something that was just in our heads, but was evident through Suzanne's mediumship as well.

The overall experience with Suzanne Giesemann was wonderful for both Allison and me. Suzanne brought an energy to the reading that had a very positive and lasting impact on both of us.

Continuing Messages

During my daily meditation sessions or walks in the woods, I would often connect again with Davey or other family members, usually just basking in the joy of their company. Occasionally I would even get a visit from the family member of a close friend that had passed, and their spirit would ask that I convey a message—though that could be a little awkward. Not everyone is open to receiving a message from a loved one that has transitioned, so knowing how to bring that up is a challenge.

Five months to the day after my dad had transitioned I was taking a walk in the woods and thinking again about my father. As I walked along the trail I had a vision of my dad. It was clear to me that I was seeing his actual transition out of this physical world and his entrance into the afterlife. I stopped in my tracks and began to take it in.

He was standing in an open space, facing away from me, though I clearly knew it was my father. I was floating above and behind him, and I felt others next to me, watching this unfold. A large crowd of people came into focus in front of him, though I couldn't see their faces, just the outlines of their bodies. They seemed to have an ethereal, glowing quality around them. As they moved closer to him I could see that the first person to greet him was my mother. She came forward and embraced my dad. As she did so, her glow seemed to light up my father with the same color that surrounded her.

I then could see both of my grandmothers there too, along with other family members. As each of them moved forward, I could see them embracing my dad. Deep down I knew what was happening; I was seeing this unfold from my soul's higher self. Suddenly I felt an extraordinary move through my physical body. It was so ght I was going to explode and the images I y disappeared.

had read about the afterlife stated that physical bodies simply cannot contain the entirety of our energy. I felt that just for that brief moment I had been exposed to my soul's full energy and it was nearly overwhelming.

I was back to standing in the middle of the forest, my heart pounding and my breath ragged, as though I had been running at full speed. It took me a few minutes to compose myself and continue my walk, but again, the feelings of connectedness to my family remained with me.

All of these experiences pushed Allison and me to continue exploring spirituality in different ways, and we soon found ourselves at a weekend workshop put on by Hay House publishers in the city of Toronto. John Holland, a famous medium, was hosting an all-day session called Magic of the Soul, which we signed up for. The session was designed to help the attendees find different ways to see our souls shine through, and hundreds of people were in the audience. Allison and I arrived pretty early and secured seats just a few rows back from the stage.

John has a tremendously funny and engaging style, and laughter frequently punctuated the session. In one exercise early on, he asked that each of us write down a person that we looked up to and then, under their name, write down the attributes of that person that made us hold them in such high regard.

After we were all finished writing, John looked around the audience to ask for examples of what people had written down. Since the audience was predominantly female I apparently stood out, and he asked me to give my response. A microphone was handed to me and I nervously answered:

"The person I most look up to is my wife." I nodded my head toward Allison and the entire audience broke out into "awwww" sounds. I proceeded to turn beet-red, my usual response to being put in the spotlight.

"The reasons are her examples of love, her kindness, her generosity, the example she provides for our children...I could just keep going, but you get the idea."

John told me that was a smart answer. He spoke for a minute about those qualities, then suddenly shifted gears.

He said, "I normally don't do readings during this, at least not this early in the day, but there is a presence around you that wants you to know that he's here. Is your father on the other side?"

I answered yes and he quickly continued in a rapid series of statements that he asked that I confirm:

"He is telling me that you have three kids, one and two."

Yes, a boy and two girls.

"You have just one brother."

Yes.

"You have two houses and are considering a third."

Yes. Allison and I have been talking for years about getting a home in Florida when we retire.

"You have a May anniversary."

Yes.

"He says he is very proud of you."

Again, this was something my dad always said to me.

"He is a fun guy with a cool energy. He says he was also an alcoholic, but a nice one, unlike my dad, who was a mean drunk."

Yes, this was of course true. John Holland explained that his father was also an alcoholic, but very violent, and it made John's childhood very difficult.

This little reading took all of about a minute and then John moved on, going back to asking other audience members about who they looked up to and why. It was the only reading he gave that morning, focusing instead on the primary purpose of the class, which was better understanding our souls.

Within about thirty minutes of the reading we got our first break of the morning and we all got up to stretch our legs. I immediately went out into the hallway to call my brother, Daryl in California to tell him that our dad had just come through in a reading. As I related the details to Daryl he said I would not believe what had happened to *him* just half an hour earlier, at about the same time our reading was going on.

Daryl had turned on his TV in the family room and it was on the same cable movie channel he had been watching the night before. It was in the middle of an old movie made in 1957, with Robert Mitchum playing a US Marine shipwrecked on an island with a nun as his only companion. As Daryl grabbed the remote to change the channel he heard some dialogue from the movie and the line "Hello, Mr. Allison."

He watched for a few minutes before pulling up the TV's guide, where he saw the name of the movie:
Heaven Knows, Mr. Allison.

We both got that tingly feeling that is often associated with a spiritual connection and marveled at how our dad was reaching out to both of us at the same time in two completely different places.

I continue to receive messages from my family on the other side on a regular basis. Knowing they are still very much a part of my life has helped make everything that I experience here in this physical world much easier.

Transformations

In the time since Davey transitioned into the afterlife I've noticed a profound transformation in myself. Not only do I now accept that there is an afterlife, I use this perspective to alter the way I approach relationships, my view of myself, and how I consider virtually everything in life. Every single change has been positive and has helped me learn to live a much happier existence. The majority of these changes have been internal, and have required that I rewire my own brain a bit, to change my perspective and allow me to see things in a new light.

I believe this transformation has been critical to my healing, because one of the first questions I had in reference to myself after my son passed was "Will I ever be happy again?" Up until that point in time I had lived a very happy life—and as any engineer will tell you, if it ain't broke, don't fix it. The most obvious solution was to return to my happy state as quickly as possible, patching up the gaping hole in the middle of my life and returning to my previously scheduled programming.

When software engineers discover that a system has a major problem, they often use one of two ways to solve it: quickly develop a patch or rebuild a larger portion of the system, in order to address the problem at its core. While I may have been able to just patch this problem up—work through the sadness and learn to avoid anything that reminded me of my loss—I chose instead to take this as the life lesson it appeared to be and to rebuild myself completely.

Spirituality

After Davey entered the afterlife, I became obsessed with connecting to him on the other side. I desperately wanted to feel his presence and I accomplished that in a deep and meaningful way. Not just believing but *knowing* that my son was fine and still a part of my life became a tremendous source of relief from the loss of his physical presence.

Initially, having a connection to Davey in his spiritual form was like having him be a toddler again. I needed to know where he was regularly, and every time I went into meditation it was to connect with him and feel his spiritual presence. I viewed it as an extension of being his parent, wanting to know that he was okay.

But I soon started to realize that it wasn't my son that was the toddler; it was me. Our roles had been reversed and now it was my son that was helping me grow spiritually. He had already ascended to the next plane; it was me still back here in the physical world, grasping for his hand and seeking constant validation that he was a part of my life.

Over time I stopped feeling compelled to reach out to Davey every chance I got, because I knew he was there if I really needed him, and as part of my own growth I didn't want to lean on him. Instead I started to explore other aspects of spirituality, from connecting with my guides to connecting to nature at a more energetic level. Once I started to look at everything as energy and not matter, my perspective allowed me to view things differently.

This was a subtle shift. I didn't suddenly see everything as though I was in the movie *The Matrix*, with shimmering energy streams everywhere. For me this didn't happen in a visual way, only in the way I now processed things. I felt more connected than I ever had to every single thing.

At this point in my life, I still find myself dropping into my old views pretty easily, but it gets easier and easier to recognize when that happens and recalibrate my perspective.

Mindfulness

Modern life, especially for technology-oriented people like me, is full of diversions. I had to learn to quiet the constant chatter of my mind and the squirrel-like attention span that accompanied me in every waking moment. Combine that with being an entrepreneur, and my life prior to this journey was fraught with an overwhelming number of distractions that came up again and again.

If modern life moves fast, the high-tech space moves at warp speed, and keeping an eye on trends and directions as well as changes in the marketplace requires a thumb on the pulse of dozens of different news feeds. Throw in a heavy dose of divisive politics, popular news media that only seem to be able to monetize outrage, and social networking platforms that create unrealistic views of life, and it's easy to get overwhelmed by the information available. Finally, take all of that and make it accessible on a mobile device that goes with you everywhere, and it's easy to see how this can put a thought stream into overdrive.

It wasn't until grief virtually shut down my usual thoughts that I was able to even recognize this as a problem. As the severe pain of the grief started to subside and the thoughts began to return I was able to head that off before I went back to my old way of life. I didn't want to return to letting my thoughts run rampant and simply resign myself to living a distracted life.

Taking up meditation gave me a powerful tool to better direct my thoughts, and more important, select which thoughts I actually wanted to embrace. The thoughts still came up, but I learned how to simply let them go and focus on what was in front of me instead of engaging them. It was the start of becoming more mindful.

Walks in the woods became opportunities to see flora and fauna in a completely new way, to breathe the air deeply and feel all of my senses come alive — rather than simply recycling the same old thoughts over and over again. My work improved, because I found I was able to focus more intently and not be pulled away by doubts about approaches to solving a problem. My relationships became much deeper, whether with family, friends, or business associates.

Through mindfulness I learned to be a better listener, not feeling compelled to interrupt someone during a conversation because I wanted to make a point. I tried to stop forming a response to what someone was telling me, while they were telling me. Instead I focused my attention on their words, visual clues, and the energy they sent out. I was even able to let those random thoughts like "I need to cut sugar out of my diet" fly by like street signs on a familiar road.

In short, I stopped defining myself as my thoughts, and started to see them as just another sensory input that I could now choose to ignore.

Judgment

While I feel that I've always been a nice person outwardly, I wasn't always nice on the inside. I would occasionally judge other people, usually just in my thoughts, but sometimes in my words to others. While I would never say out loud "Whoa, you need to cut out the junk food" or "Have some self respect, man," I would think these things.

I learned that how I thought, not just about myself but about other people, directly impacted the quality of the relationships I had. It was like turning on a light switch and seeing something for the first time, but this time it was people that suddenly lit up for me.

The negative or critical thoughts I had of other people stopped being voiceless and harmless words that simply rose and fell behind my eyes. I realized that every thought I had about other people became a piece of energy, packaged up and shot like a rocket at the very person I was judging. I was no longer able to hide behind the veil of my internal thoughts—I realized that I was completely transparent. Every thought I had of other people, both while in their presence and remotely, was accessible to that person if they were paying attention. While this may sound terrifying, it was ultimately a wonderful gift, once I recognized the benefits of seeing people through this new lens.

Initially I simply replaced my harsher internal judgments with kinder thoughts: "Well, she has a nice smile" and "He's making the best of a bad situation." This was an improvement, but the judgment was still there. Instead, I sought to be as nonjudgmental as possible, focusing on only one thing in other people: *this person is the same as I am.* They come from the same Source I do, but with their own challenges and needs. I don't know exactly what they need right now, but there's one thing I know everyone can use: loving acknowledgment.

By simply looking at people with loving attention, I found myself in a completely different world. Other people were now partners in this dance of life. In their eyes I saw a lifetime of joys and challenges, and I appreciated that they were still here and for a brief moment in time were right in front of me, exposing their soul to mine.

The clerk at the mini-market register looked like she was having a difficult day, and sullenly told me the total for my purchase. I looked into her eyes and focused on sending loving attention her way, asking if she was okay. "I'm supposed to be over there changing out the coffee, but I can't because people keep coming up to the register...." I smiled and told her "I'm sorry, that's my fault, but I really appreciate you working today and helping me out." She quickly returned the smile and I could see her face brighten. We exchanged "Have a nice day!" at the same time and laughed.

Every day, my life includes little interactions like this. People are no longer background extras that fulfill some machine-like function while I go through life, even if they have that detached, mechanical expression as they interact with me. There is a light within every single person and I have found that if I look into a person's eyes with loving attention and acknowledgment, that light shines through.

Initially, it took a lot of focus to allow this to be my default behavior, but now that it is, it has become my habitual way of encountering other people.

Death and Dying

My view of my own mortality has also changed rather dramatically. I wouldn't say that I feared death before, but I always viewed it as a negative event that I didn't want to think about. On the rare occasion that I was challenged to consider my own demise, I wanted it to happen on my terms: I would live a long and productive life. In my final days I would know that my time was near, my extensive group of friends and family would gather by my bedside and bid me a final farewell, and I would simply drift off in my sleep — without any pain — to whatever came next.

I knew I couldn't escape death, but I was willing to consider it on my own terms.

Because I was so centered and focused on this life I'm living, it defined every aspect of my existence. Prior to Davey's passing I never even considered that I had existed before my own physical birth, and the only thing I felt confident would survive my physical death were my children. In part that's why they became such a big part of my focus; I didn't know what came next but since my children would outlive me, that meant some part of me would continue.

That is, until one of them didn't.

I lost my fear of death the day my son died. Initially it was because I was in so much pain that death didn't seem like such a bad thing. I wasn't suicidal, but saw death more as a sweet release than the ominous feeling it used to present. I knew that I had a lot of other people counting on me, especially my wife and daughters, and that was the one thing that seemed to give me purpose initially.

As my spiritual awareness grew from a curiosity to a belief system to a knowing, the concept of my own death took on a different meaning. It stopped being about the end, and more about the beginning of a new phase, one that was now important to my spiritual growth. I started to see that there wasn't a "good" death, nor was there a "bad" death. It's simply the punctuation mark at the end of a sentence and my full story is a significantly longer one.

In the context of a soul's journey I see every life, from one that is incredibly short to those that last beyond a century, as a beautiful and complete life that can be celebrated. The impact

that every life has on others is profound, and the wa͟
viewed each of those lives was my choice.

As a result, I also handle the news of someone else's death
very differently now. When presented with the news that
someone has passed that isn't a friend or relative of the person
bearing the news, I don't drop into the old "That's horrible…"
or "What a shame…" I simply acknowledge it, letting the
bearer know that I had or had not heard that news. If the
person bearing the news is very close to the recently deceased,
I focus on sending love and attention to the person bearing the
burden of grief. The only thing I try to convey to them is that I
am willing to help however they need it and that I'm thinking
of them.

I try not to impress my belief system on them, focusing
instead on being an example of peace and happiness, even
though I've been exposed to loss that I never thought I could
recover from.

Getting Through Each Day

All of these changes have helped me navigate my daily life
much more easily. The changes in my perspective have helped
me silence the thoughts that kept me from sleeping at night.
Every morning starts with a healthy breakfast and a
meditation session that usually lasts about thirty minutes. If I
struggle to get "into the zone" during my meditation, I
practice gratitude.

I've learned to truly love myself as I am right now, at this
moment. I see myself as the sum of all of my experiences, not
the sum of my accomplishments. My ego has learned to
become a partner in this journey, not the dominant part of my
personality, consumed with vanity. When my ego tries to
insult or belittle me because of something I did poorly, I

ive it and move on, not allowing it to continue

my daily exercise include some form of outdoor
, especially since the majority of my working hours are
spent inside a climate-controlled environment. When I am
outside, I'm constantly in awe of the nature of our world,
appreciating all of the complex interactions that need to
happen for something as small as a blade of grass to grow into
the tiny object I see before me.

My body is now more a temple than the definition of my
existence. Just because I view myself as an immortal soul
doesn't mean that I can simply ignore my body. This body of
mine is the vehicle for my experiences and needs to be
respected and maintained, both mentally and physically. I do
this not to make my body last as long as possible, but to allow
me to experience life through as many possibilities as I can.

I no longer need the constant distraction of music or talking
heads to occupy my time during long drives in the car. Simply
focusing on my driving and allowing my mind to take a break
is now a welcome experience.

Finally, since Davey is still very much a part of my life, I
frequently talk about him to others. I don't hesitate at all to tell
people that I have three children. With friends and family I'm
always comfortable saying things like "Davey loved going to
Candy Kitchen" or "Davey would love that." Often when I
say things like that I'll hear Davey in my thoughts say "I do
love that, Dad."

I tend to gloss over some things when I speak to new people
that don't know about Davey, at least initially. I still
acknowledge my son and will even talk about him in
generalities, but I will never imply that he hasn't transitioned.
If a new acquaintance probes deep enough I will gently

disclose that we lost him in a traffic accident and gauge their response.

I do this not because I don't want to discuss that part of Davey's life, but to save the other person from the cognitive dissonance that comes up when they realize this happy person in front of then has been talking about a child that has passed.

Epilogue

When I set out on this journey I was obsessed with finding my son, hoping that doing so would heal the intense pain I felt and give me some answers.

Along the way, I not only found my son, but also my father. Understanding the complex role he played in my life and how it had helped me be a father to my own children was an important moment for me.

It wasn't, however, until I found my father's son that I was able to get the answers I sought. Learning who I really am, the role I play in this existence, and experiencing all that life has to offer has helped me embrace everything with a deep love and reverence that I never felt before.

Knowing—not just believing—that I am more than just a physical body that will break down and die one day opens a tremendous opportunity to view life through a new lens. When the stresses of modern life start to crop up, I see them from a very different angle. Even things that in the past would trigger a negative reaction from me become learning experiences and I now embrace them.

This doesn't mean I have become a passive individual that is simply trampled over by others, sitting back and allowing life to happen to me. Far from it. I'm now able to see the events that caused storms of thought to swirl in my mind, and pull back from them to make clearer choices. I don't feel the need to incite storms of thought in other people's lives, simply to feel validated about the tempest brewing between my temples. I just see it and let it go.

If I could give you one gift, it would be to see yourself as I now see people. A beautiful soul on an endless journey of vast experiences. Every challenge in life is just an event on that journey, a lesson that helps you become more complete. You are truly amazing!

There is one memory I go back to frequently. It is the day of my son's accident and his physical time on this planet would be complete in just a few hours. I'm sitting in the big chair on our screened-in porch, deeply troubled by the events of the past few days and intensely worried about my son.

Davey opens the sliding glass door and comes outside. He leans over and hugs me, pressing the side of his face against mine, and says, "It's okay, Dad, I'm right here. I'll never leave you! I will always be with you!"

He's been with me ever since, it just took me some time to truly believe it.

30259731R00081

Printed in Poland
by Amazon Fulfillment
Poland Sp. z o.o., Wrocław